This Book is Humbly Dedicated to

The Divine Lotus Feet

of

Lord Shri Krishna

The Motivator of the Entire Universe

Whose Love Inspired me to

Complete the Task Undertaken

EDUCATION FOR VALUES

Dr. USHA RAO
M.A. (Phil.), M.A. (Psy.), M.Ed., Ph.D.
Former Principal,
Gokhale Education Society's
College of Education and Research
Parel, Mumbai 400 012.

First Edition : 2011

Himalaya Publishing House

MUMBAI • NEW DELHI • NAGPUR • BENGALURU • HYDERABAD • CHENNAI • PUNE • LUCKNOW • AHMEDABAD • ERNAKULAM • BHUBANESWAR • INDORE • KOLKATA

First Edition : 2011

Published by : Mrs. Meena Pandey for **Himalaya Publishing House Pvt. Ltd.,** "Ramdoot", Dr. Bhalerao Marg, Girgaon, **Mumbai - 400 004.** Phone: 022 - 2386 01 70/2386 38 63, Fax: 022-2387 71 78 **Email: himpub@vsnl.com Website: www.himpub.com**

Branch Offices:

New Delhi : "Pooja Apartments", 4-B, Murari Lal Street, Ansari Road, Darya Ganj, New Delhi - 110 002. Phone: 011 - 23270392, 23278631 Fax: 011-23256286

Nagpur : Kundanlal Chandak Industrial Estate, Ghat Road, Nagpur - 440 018. Phone: 2738731, 3296733 Telefax: 0712-2721215

Bengaluru : No. 16/1 (Old 12/1), 1st Floor, Next to Hotel Highlands, Madhava Nagar, Race Course Road, Bengaluru - 560 001. Phone: 080 - 2281541, 22385461, Telefax: 080-22286611

Hyderabad : No. 3-4-184, Lingampally, Besides Raghavendra Swamy Matham, Kachiguda, Hyderabad - 500 027. Phone: 040-27560041, 27550139, Mobile: 09848130433

Chennai : No. 85/50, Bazullah Road, T. Nagar, Chennai - 600 017. Phone: 044-28144004/28144005

Pune : First Floor, "Laksha" Apartment, No. 527, Mehunpura, Shaniwarpeth (Near Prabhat Theatre), Pune - 411 030. Phone: 020-24496323/24496333

Lucknow : Jai Baba Bhavan, Church Road, Near Manas Complex and Dr. Awasthi Clinic, Aliganj, Lucknow - 226 024. Phone: 0522-2339329, 4068914, Mobile: 9305302158, 9415349385, 9389593752

Ahmedabad : 114, "SHAIL", 1st Floor, Opp. Madhu Sudan House, C.G.Road, Navrang Pura, Ahmedabad - 380 009. Phone: 079-26560126, Mobile: 09327324149, 09314679413

Ernakulam : 39/104 A, Lakshmi Apartment, Karikkamuri Cross Rd., Ernakulam, Cochin - 622011, Kerala. Phone: 0484-2378012, 2378016, Mobile: 09344199799

Bhubaneswar : 5 Station Square, Bhubaneswar (Odisha) - 751 001. Mobile: 9861046007

Indore : Kesardeep Avenue Extension, 73, Narayan Bagh, Flat No. 302, IIIrd Floor, Near Humpty Dumpty School, Narayan Bagh, Indore 452 007(M.P.) Mobile: 09301386468

Kolkata : 108/4, Beliaghata Main Road, Near ID Hospital, Opp. SBI Bank, Kolkata - 700 010, Mobile: 09910440956

DTP by : (Apte)

Printed by : A to Z Printer, New Delhi.

PREFACE

"ALL EYES SEEM TO SET ON EDUCATION"

It is very true!

The contemporary scene of India compels each one to turn to education as the central key to the road of regeneration. Unfortunately, our educational system is suffering from long standing negligence and maladies and unless drastic steps are taken to bring about radical and revolutionary changes, it would be futile to expect education to perform any miracle. It is at this juncture, a temptation has arised to quote an incident in the life of Rabindranath Tagore. When he was a boy, his eyes were weak. But, he did not know that his situation was abnormal. He saw things rather blurred and indistinct, but he thought that was the way things were seen, until one day, in jest, he took a playmate's spectacles and tried them out. For the first time in life, Rabindranath saw clearly, neatly, distinctly. He could now see far off things too with perfect clarity and near with absolute perfection. This experience stayed with him for life and even reflected in his understanding of life. Somewhat same thing has happened today. We are witnessing today the curse of indiscipline spreading in all sections of the society. Because of this we all have an inditinct and blurred vision. However, such existing circumstances has forced we people working in the field of education to view things in perfect clarity. Our own experiences on various occasions have made us aware of and forced us to reflect on certain essential features of life that can be treasured and termed 'VALUE'.

Education can never be complete unless it equips the individual for meeting challenges of life and also prepares him or her to shoulder the moral responsibilities. During the last four decades, the main focus has been on the quantitative expansion, and consequently, adequate attention has not been paid on maintaining standards and quality of education.

A question is often asked as to what are the immediate yardsticks for determining what has come to be called 'Qualitative Education'. It may be answered that it is only when contents and methods of education inspire every child to surpass his or her limitations, that, the quality of education attains its distinctiveness. 'Quality Education' promotes excellence amongst students, both individally and collectively.

While going through the above discussions, a fact to note is that instead of helping the students to develop correct meaning and correct purpose of life, education has placed them in such an environment where they are disoriented and accordingly, it has developed a sort of disregard for the consideration of values. And, education that is not value-oriented is anything but education! Value oriented education is that education which aims at making students good citizens who may share their responsibilities in the changing set of society, in order to to give a desired shape and image to the society and community at large.

National Policy on Education, 1986 envisages, “A human being is a positive asset and a precious national resource which need to be cherished, nurtured and developed.” Essence of education is to develop the human personality in all its dimensions — intellectual, physical, social, moral and spiritual. But, out of these, development of values has not been attended properly.

Development of values in pupils is a difficult task; and Value-education must start from the very beginning, because, at a very young age we have to start to inculcate the values and social norms of the society. Hence, it is a teacher who should have a sound psychological knowledge of different qualities that come into play in various actions and of the right laws of the development of personality in relation to the development of capacities and values of an integrated personality. The concept of value-oriented educational pattern requires a great professional competency on the part of the teacher to mould the strength and behaviour of pupils. To enable them to assume new roles in an efficient manner requires special training. The existing system appears to be static and rigid to cope with the new situations existing in the society. Therefore, a sound prorgramme of professional education of teachers is very much essential for the qualitative improvement of education.

For the last two decades, I had been reading and thinking about value-education, and also meeting many teachers, administrators and also researchers who used to be always involved in the task of planning, doing and studying value-education. The strong expression that was gained was that VALUE-EDUCATION is regarded as a cure and prevention for certain social problems. It was, therefore, thought that value-education could really contribute to encouraging behaviour appropriate to the well being of all in an initial way considered this to be equivalent to curing and preventing certain social problems. Accordingly, the main intention of bringing out this small book was to present a few examples of how VALUE EDUCATION PROGRAMME (VEPs) help, cure and prevent certain social problems and to explain why they have greater success than other programmes. But, despite many firm reasons, why value-education should help, cure and prevent social problems, and strong claims that it does, somehow or other, I really had difficulty of finding evidence to support the claims.

On the basis of the above said facts it was anticipated that some value-education approaches would not be called ‘value-education’ and it would be essential to justify the selection of each instance used as value-education approach. Secondly, the term 'cure' does not mean 'total cure'. For example, evidence of a cure would be reduction of the problem of a particular group of people being favourably influenced so as not to contribute to the problem. It was, therefore, realised, that, a sort of more adequate expression of the title to this book would be "EDUCATION FOR VALUES". Next, while some immature and unsocialised behaviour may really attribute to a social problem, this does not mean that all such behaviour does. Consequently, the possible inter relationship of value-education, immature behaviour and social problems would have to be very carefully explained. With this background, a sincere attempt has been made here in bringing about this book. Over and above, being working in Teacher's Training College, in the capacity of a lecturer for some years and also as a principal of the College, it was felt very much honestly that first of all, our teacher-trainees should be well trained as would be teachers of 'VALUE EDUCATION' and its concept, would really suffice the matter. Our teacher-trainees are would be teachers. It is they, who should be helped to draw a clear concept regarding value-education. Hence, they must be made to learn, understand and get well-versed in handling the most important ten values laid down by the Government of Maharashtra for inculcating the same in schools. Now, when our teacher-trainees enter the teaching profession, the handling of the subject of value-education will not be felt difficult by them and the assigned tasks will work out smoothly. It is at this juncture, that, having set the mind to think in the said direction, I have ventured in attempting to include the chapter entitled 'VALUE-ORIENTED TEACHER-EDUCATION', wherein, a responsibility and work of Teachers' Training Colleges has been discussed in details. Much has been viewed about the handling of the topic of 'Value-Education' by teacher-trainees when they actually enter the profession chosen by them.

A short description of important concept of values in education and few important details of significant schemes of imparting values in schools have also been discussed.

I am indeed indebted to HIMALAYA PUBLICATION for giving me the required encouragement to write the book on EDUCATION FOR VALUES and also for bringing out this book in the market. I also thanks to the typist, the B.Ed. student-teachers, and few principals of the schools for their good support in completing the project undertaken. In fact, all the heads, hands and hearts come together, had made me successful in bringing out this book, which is purely written with the intention of providing the teachers with the variety of ideas, approaches and techniques which can be utilised by them in a proper perspective.

Values and the teaching strategies associated with it are presented in the current book. Although preliminary research shows it to be especially potent for those children who suffer from value confusion, it is doubtlessly appropriate for all children living in today's complex world.

I am always thankful to my learned readers who are sure to go through this book. If they have any suggestions to offer, I shall definitely like to have for my future use.

LAST BUT NOT THE LEAST, MY THANKS TO THE ALMIGHTY IN GIVING ME PHYSICAL AS WELL AS MENTAL STRENGTH FOR WRITHING THIS BOOK.

Dr. USHA RAO

CONTENTS

INTRODUCTION 1

The greatest need of today is that man in his mad race in pursuit of transient materialistic gains and objectives, should, at least, occasionally pause and reflect on the real purpose and values of human life, and give a fresh orientation to his or her view of life based on such introspective reflection. If this were done, one should have absolutely no difficulty to realise that amongst all living species, the human being occupies a special and exalted place by reason of his or her alone being endowed with powers of reason and also discrimination aided by a discerning intellect and faculties of analytical thinking, assimilation and recollection. From time immemorial, these special gifts have generated in man a keen sense of inquiry in search of truth, wisdom and bliss — "SAT, CHIT, ANAND".

The most precious asset possessed by our country is our glorious ancient culture firmly founded on the principles of SANATANA DHARAMA. This culture has been handled down from generation to generation during the past thousands of years and it lies embedded in the hearts and souls of the millions of the people belonging to different religious faiths that are knit together by this common cultural bond.

In the above said connection, it is too much felt to quote the following prayer —

सर्वे सन्तु सुखिनः
सर्वे सन्तु निरामयाः
सर्वे भद्राणि पश्चन्तुः
मा काश्चित् दुःखभागे भवंतुः

Let all be happy.

Let all be healthy.

Let all be gentle.

Let none have sorrow.

This is what an Indian prays — when he or she prays for his or her well-being as per the teachings of the Ancient Munis and Rishis. How very true! Unless the training given to our children is such as to acqaint them with the fundamentals of the glorious ancient culture of India and develop in their minds a deep and abiding respect for all faiths as well as a clean sense of pride about our unique cultural heritage, the preservation of our cultural heritage will be seriously in peril.

Under the educational system which is currently in vogue in our country, the emphasis is solely on the imparting of knowledge that is concerned with the academic subjects included in the curriculum and no attention is usually paid to the development of the child's character and inner personality. The result is that children grow up without getting any opportunity to know about the glorious cultural traditions of our country and great moral and spiritual values on which the culture is based. Student-power, today, is not harnessed collectively for attainment of social harmony and well-being. The restlessness that has lately polluted the atmosphere of our educational institutions is undoubtedly the result of a social-sickness that has seized the Indian Youth on account of their innermost cultural aspirations having remained unheeded. It is only when they are enabled to plunge into the depths of their own souls and pursue the quest of discovering the DIVINE in each human heart will be drawn towards establishing themselves as members of a society based on pure and unselfish love and untinted mutual co-operation. For this, it is really very much necessary that an opportunity should be provided to the students to acquaint themselves with the basic features of our glorious, spiritual and cultural heritage which, with its essential qualities, cuts as under all sorts of distinctions of caste, community, race and religion and underlines the brotherhood of man and the fatherhood of God. Such broad-based education will prompt the students to devote every minute of activity of theirs for the pilgrimage to God within themselves through the path of selfless service to fellowmen. Such an integrated process of correcting and shaping the child's attitudes and reactions will mould them into ideal citizens most useful to the society, befitting our great traditions.

Of all the countries in the world, we, in India, have the richest cultural as well as spiritual heritage. But it is a sad irony of fate that ever since we attained our Independence, we have been denying the youth of this country even the barest opportunity to imbibe the great moral, cultural as well as spiritual values that form part of his or her heritage by imposing a taboo on all moral and spiritual institutions in the name of secularism. There cannot be a greater type of misunderstanding of the importance of secularism.

The Kothari Commission Report published in 1966 laid the highest stress on the need for moral and spiritual education and it is very rightly pointed out that the modernisation of education has to derive its strength from the strength of the spirit and many serious social and ethical conflicts that are caused nowadays in society on account of the weakening of the moral values in the younger generation which can be remedied only by balancing the knowledge and skills which science and technology bring with the values and insights associated with ethics and religion as its best.

Even though nearly more than thirty years have passed since the Commission made its report, we are yet to see any action being taken by the Central and State Governments and by the Universities in India for the implementation of the most wholesome recommendations of the Commission. However, there is a silver lining in this gloomy sky which holds great hope and promise for the future. Fortunately a massive programme of providing ideal value-oriented education has been launched now since last three years by the Maharashtra State Government.

If the very concept of 'VALUE' is to be made known to the student world in the true sense of the term, then, the schools must start on the said line. It is with this view, Maharashtra State has introduced the subject of 'Value Education' and also implementing various activities in the concerned subjects right from Std. I to Std. X. Accordingly, a book on 'Education For Values' and a Handbook for Teachers has come out. Further, in all the schools of Maharashtra State, the very first period has been utilised in the regular school time-table for implementation of value-education, and also the activities connected to the value-education.

On the basis of the above said facts it is equally important for the teachers to play their roles properly. The emphasis on education for inculcation of values imposes on the teachers a very special responsibility. In this connection, one of the well-known poet's following lines are very strongly remembered.

These lines are as follows:

WHERE IS LIFE? LOST IN WISDOM!

WHERE IS WISDOM? LOST IN KNOWLEDGE!

WHERE IS KNOWLEDGE? LOST IN INFORMATION!

How very true! It is now completely the teacher's responsibility to mould the unripe minds in a proper fashion by the inculcation of values. A little penetration into the malaise and some familiarity with the student population world really indicate that things fortunately are still not beyond the stage of no return. If there are a few who adopt an unreasonable or unethical approach, there are many who have not yet succumbed. It is this innocent majority who would be concentrated upon. Schools have their own Boy-Scouts and Girl-Guides. Certain schools (of the higher secondary level) do organic blood donation drives. There are visits to slum areas too at times.

The handicapped students receive help from their fellow mates. Hiking, sports, extra-curricular activities attract a sizeable number, though not very many. These students and others are our hope and our mainstay. Besides, there are many, who in their personal lives, attend with a sincere devotion talks delivered by learned men, swamis and saints and endeavour to live upto the essence therein stressed. When the land is thus somewhat bright, when these students have not wholly forgotten our cultural heritage, we may succeed in bringing them back to the old moorings suitably altered to modern times and needs without sacrificing any of the essentials.

The primary concern of education is to explore how we may best function in universal evolution. A dedicated experienced teacher can widen the scope of the curriculum and make his or her instructions pragmatic and functional. We might have achieved education for all but let us have education for each! It is here again much can be spoken about the burning issue. Basically, values are the person's emotions and hence they are to be experienced and maximum of experience a child may gain is through education. It is through education a change must take place totally in one's behaviour. But, side by side, environment too is the most effective factor in man's education. School is the most effective environment for a growing child.

Values like love, kindness, tolerance have been practised even by the animal and bird kingdom in its intimate face to face primary group or herd and flock relationships. It is only human beings who have given wide concepts to these values to be translated into practice beyond the intimate primary group to the whole Human Society. It is because of such a concept that we call these Human values.

Values are the essence of life. They are defined as morals which build a character of human beings. Men of character build a disciplined community that provides the nation with political leadership, active and alert administrative personnel, wise parents, enthusiastic teachers and responsible citizens — who all in turn develop a strong and progressive nation.

For all the above said facts, education is the media and is the only vital medium to imbibe, foster and perpetuate values in the younger generation. It activates the latent capacities of the individual to recognise the truth, duty and goodness that is lying behind. The half-marks of an individual's personality are self-determination, self-realisation, self-integration, social adjustment, economic self-reliance and moral and social attitudes towards others. And all is achieved through value-education. It is the value-education that is helpful in developing in the child a fearlessness of mind, strength of consciousness and integrity of the purpose. But what is witnessed today? People are fighting for recognition, fanaticism and sectarianism. The young as well as an adult are still ignorant of values in the true sense of the term. Education of mind and heart is still absent. Therefore, there is a need today to have a tentative programme of value-education in schools, because the process of education is un-ending and in a real sense process of education is to humanise humanity! If we stand back and think, we notice, we have a lot to learn from the past.

As such, being a social animal, for every man, understanding of our fellow beings is important. But this understanding becomes fruitful only when it is sustained by sympathetic feeling in joy and sorrow. Therefore, a positive aspiration and effort for an ethical, moral configuration of our common life is of great importance. Without ethical culture, there is no solution to humanity. A man's ethical behaviour, is, in fact, based effectively on sympathy, education and social ties and needs. But all this is or can be achieved only by the corresponding values as these are the prime motivating force behind his or her thought, emotion and action. It is indeed unthinkable to have education without any kind of values. All educational philosophies, therefore, essentially put a stress on values. But values are not static as our relationship to this world is not static.

Today mankind is obviously in a difficult position. The difficulties have been created because of the wrong values existing in the environment which is fast changing. The time has come for everyone to think and bring about a drastic change in the educational institutions in general and in the Teachers' Training Colleges in particular. This would be possible only when the educational institutions start educating the future citizens for a new emerging ethics — the ethics of Universal Brotherhood. Like electric current which is invisible and yet can drive large mechanical equipment, a thought and an idea can produce tremendous effect. The process of education being dealing with thoughts, ideas, mind and intellect, require very careful handling and it can turn humanity either into diviity or animality.

It is because of the above said facts, it is very necessary that the Teachers' Training Colleges must start giving training to the pupil-teachers in value-education. The pupil-teachers are the would be teachers and once they are well-trained, it will become very easy for them to handle the the unriped minds when they join the teaching profession. Hence, in order to make education responsive to the needs of the society, teacher education has to be reoriented in its aim and approach, curriculum and content. It is Dr. Radhakrishnan and Rabindranath Tagore — both who may be labelled as the modern examples of great teachers — influenced this country with the philosophy of value-oriented education. Hence, it may be said again here that it is the teacher educators from the Teachers' Training Colleges who should train well their pupil teachers because when these would be teachers will start working as teachers in their respective schools they

(*a*) will have a unique position.

(*b*) will have a key to knowledge.

(*c*) will be possessing multiplier effect.

(*d*) will have a social prestige.

(*e*) will provide a model to younger generation.

Because of the above said discussion, it is very essential that teachers under training should be thoroughly exposed to values in their colleges of education. It also accordingly, presupposes that the teacher-educators also have a serious commitment to human values in life. They should not merely be good lecturers of philosophy or sociology or psychology of methodology, expert in one method or another, but they should also know the higher purpose of education and especially teacher training which, today, is on the threshold of social change and development. Hence, the transformation of education must be a collective and democratic enterprise involving the active participation of all concerned mobilising the energies and faith of teachers, teacher educators, students, parents and administrators. It needs deep vision and dynamic leadership to make education relevant to our time and capabale of meeting the challenges of the emerging future. Hence, value-orientation should be one of the main objectives of education to develop an integrated persoanlity of the student so that he or she contributes his or her best to the country. The very content of education is to be value-oriented, because every knowledge is turned into value no sooner it is applied in life. This, the term 'VALUE' covers the entire domain of the development of integrated personality through various capacities such as —

(*a*) Values of health,

(*b*) Values of courage,

(*c*) Values of clarity,

(*d*) Values of honesty,

(*e*) Values like kindness, politeness etc.

It is the children who relish observing the habits of their peer group, their teachers, their parents and then classify them into groups — Good and Bad. Their direction is always roaming in the outer world. This habit pollutes their minds. By gathering the evils of others, the mind is transformed into a newspaper which prides itself on descriptions of vice and wickedness. Hence, children have to be saved from this malignant influence, and it is the teacher who should be ever eager to cleanse their minds. Since mind is the only instrument available for preserving and enhancing the genuine human qualities our students have to be taught to desire the good and get themselves detached from bad. If the mind is shattered, it is very difficult to reshape it into a whole. An iron plate when broken into pieces can be welded into our piece. So the teachers have to strengthen the minds of the students with good faith. Now, this can be well done by teachers in general and a well-trained teacher (who has come out from a Teachers' Training College) in particular. Hence, it is the responsibility of the teacher-educators to give proper training to their pupil-teachers. The academic environment of today is not conducive to the young generation. It is filled with vices. Educationists have been labouring to work out suitable curriculum that would help development of vaues in the unripe minds. The urgent need is therefore to give education a 'value orientation' which has been well-recognised by all.

Values, can, after all, be caught and taught. When a boy wants to learn to ride a cycle, he must undergo training. Elaborate lectures on 'how to ride a cycle' would never put him on the saddle and help him move. So too is with values. They cannot be just taught by the teachers. But they could be inculcated by examples, by training and self-training. Values are neither skills nor proficiencies to be developed on the same lines that has normally been done for skill, proficiency development, etc. in the learners. Here, once again it may be stated that Teachers' Training Colleges have to teach this aspect to the teacher-trainees so that when they actually enter into the teaching profession, they will have a correct understanding as to how values can be brought into the process of learning and academic curriculum. This is now entirely the responsibility of the teacher educators. It is felt, therefore, that the main aim of the teacher-educators is to teach to their pupil-teachers about the values of the present day world. In fact, the whole purpose must be value-teaching, and the need for this can never be overlooked. While every aspect of man's life has values, education having the greatest impact of man has the greatest value. Therefore, the job of a teacher-educator should not be just to pump the knowledge in their pupil-teachers from a vessel floating up in the air into empty vessels lying below! Every attempt has to be a sincere attempt. It is rightly said —

Good teachers make good schools,
Good schools make good students,
Good students make good citizens,
Good citizens make good nation.

Hence, value-education and devoted teachers are the backbones of the entire education system which can claim to prepare a complete man in the future.

2

HUMAN VALUES

After having read the contents of the current chapter, our reader will find that each line of every page, highlights the present scenario with regard to erosion of values in Indian Society. There is no need to emphasise the fact that the desirable values can be inculcated by or through value-oriented education. The only request to our reader is that he or she should read each line very carefully.

After going through this chapter, the reader will be able to:

- explain the need for value-oriented education in the country;
- identify the values which need to be inculcated in learners at different stages of school education; and
- classify the values which are essential for teachers.

In ancient societies, religion had a dominating influence in every sphere of human activity. Result was, the content of education was more or less religious in nature. Besides mental training, moral training was emphasised to a great extent. Learners had to undergo rigorous character training and value-education during their stay in Gurukuls or Ashrams. Much stress was on spiritual development of the teachers. THUS, THE ENTIRE EDUCATION SYSTEM WAS PRIMARILY VALUE ORIENTED!

But as the days passed by, there was a gradual erosion of values and the so-called modern education entered inside the modern world. Character training and value-education started getting ignored. Materialism, cut-throat competition, influence of Western Culture, etc. contributed a lot which resulted in all kinds of value-crisis. Newspapers were full of news like rape of minor children, kidnapping, forgery, gang-rape of gilrs/women, thefts, murder, killing of brides for dowry, etc. Vices like drinking, drugging, gambling etc. are now on increase. Thus, by all such quoted facts it is seen that a factor called 'CONTENTMENT' has started losing the ground! Corruption has entered in all walks of life.

Based on the above quoted facts one can understand the strong need for the education in human values. The process of inculcating values must start right from the primary education level. In other words, Education in Human Values need to be incorporated as an integral component of the entire educational system.

After all this discussion, the question that now jumps up like a boomerang is "WHAT IS VALUE?" Literally, value means something that has a price, and is precious. In a given situation, a person may have a number of alternative responses. However, he or she chooses one which is guided by his or her values. A value is an emotional attitude which motvates a person dirctly or indirectly to act in the most desirable way preferred by him or her. Without values, one floats like a piece of drift wood in the swirling waters of a river. Values control and guide human behaviour. Value is a norm. It is an abiding goal. For progress, vaues are needed. In our philosophic tradition, we come across the widely accepted concept of value — TRUTH, BEAUTY and GOODNESS — सत्यम, शिवम, सुंदरम.

Swami Vivekananda declared selflessness and sacrifice to be our national values in the following word:

> **"The national ideal of India are service and renunciation. Intensify her in those channels and the rest will take care of itself."**
>
> *(India and Her Problems, p. 19)*

Swami Vivekananda also observed —

"Every act of love brings happiness. There is no act of love which does not bring peace." He also said further — "Love never fails, today or tomorrow or ages after, truth will conquer and love shall win the victory."

According to Swami Vivekananda, "Education is not the amount of information that is put into your brain .... we trust to have life-building, manmaking, character-making, assimilation of ideas."

Shri Satya Sai Baba mentioned five Universal Human Value —

Satya (Truth)

Dharma (Righteous Conduct)

Shanti (Peace)

Prem (Love) and

Ahimsa (Non-violence).

The above said values Satya Sai Baba has beautifully emphasised in the following sentence —

"Truth, Righteous Conduct, Non-Violence, Peace and Love are the five life breaths of every human being. Among these five life breaths of a human being, Love has a unique place. Therefore, establish love firmly in your hearts." He has further elaborated the significance of love saying —

Love as thought is Truth,

Love as action is Righteous Conduct,

Love as feeling is Peace and

Love as understanding is Non-violence.

Gandhiji advised the inmates of Sabarmati Ashram on the practice of following values in their day-to-day life.

Ahimsa (Non-violence)

Satya (Truth)

Astheya (Non-stealing)

Brahmacharya (Chastity)

Asamvah (Non-possession)

Swadeshi (Swadeshi)

Asprushyata (Removal of Untouchability)

Shareer Shram (Manual Work)

Vrata Ashrem (Control of Palate)

Nirbheedta (Fearlessness).

Sri Aurobindo mentioned that 'education is not realised through what a person learns but what he becomes'. Aurobindo's concept of integral education has given five following components:

1. Physical,
2. Vital,
3. Mental,
4. Psychic and
5. Spiritual.

He further mentioned that these five components must continue complementing each other till the end of one's life.

The Preamble of Indian Constitution has laid emphasis on the following 4 universal values —

JUSTICE of social, economic and political;

LIBERTY of thought, expression, belief, faith, worship;

EQUALITY of status and opportunity and to promote among them all; and

FRATERNITY — assuring the dignity of the individual and the unity and integrety of the nation.

The National Policy on Education,1986 emphasized promotion of the following values —

1. India's common cultural heritage,
2. Egalitarianism, democracy and secularism,
3. Equality of the sexes,
4. Protection of the environment,
5. Removal of social barriers,
6. Observance of small family norms,
7. Inculcation of the scientific temper,
8. The Constitutional obligations,
9. Content essential to nurture national identity,
10. History of India's freedom movement.

The National Curriculum Framework for School Education (2000), highlights that the following values need to be added —

1. Human Rights including rights of the child and those of the girl child.
2. Inculcation and sustenace of Personal, Social, National and Spiritual values.

Amrik Singh (2000) mentions that certain value needed to be promoted whereas certain others are to be curbed.

Values to be promoted are:

1. Dignity of labour
2. Gender equality
3. Sense of excellence
4. Recognition of diversity in social and cultural life.

Values to be curbed are:

1. Excessive projection of violence through cinema and television,
2. Undermining of our family traditions.

Values to be included at elementary stage are:

Good manners

Orderliness

Discipline

Compassion

Cleanliness and personal hygiene

Cooperation

Honesty

Simplicity

Courage

Sense of duty and responsibility

Faithfulness

Values to be included at Secondary Stage are:

Patriotism

Dignity of labour

Justice

Human brotherhood

Democratic spirit

Respect for all religion

Humanism and love for mankind

Tolerance

International understanding

Proper utilisation of time

Dependability

Service to others

Sense of excellence

Endurance

Recognition of diversity in social life

Gender sensitivity

Scientific temper

Values to be included among teachers are:

1. Appreciating feelings of students
2. Punctuality
3. Personal hygiene
4. Cleanliness of environment
5. Modesty
6. Compassion
7. Appreciating students' ideas
8. Concern for disadvantaged children
9. Cordial relationship with colleagues
10. Honesty
11. Spirit of inquiry
12. Quest for knowledge

13. Obedience to head of institution
14. Tolerance
15. Checking home assignments properly
16. No discrimination towards children on the basis of sex, caste, creed and economic status.

Concludingly it may be said that school is the most appropriate setting for inculcation of values and teacher is the most appropriate person for inculcating the same.

3

WHAT IS A VALUE?

INTRODUCTION

Many educationists have made a sincere attempt to find out the answers to questions like —

- What do we mean by the team VALUE?
- Is value something that can be discovered in ourselves or in objects and nature around us?
- Is value content-based or global?
- Is value something that can be created?

The answers to the questions quoted above are probably dependent on our present perceptions of the nexus between man and man, between man and society, between man and the universe, between man's self and supreme-self. But what actually we are interested is to understand the concept underlying the terms 'VALUE'. Accordingly, when the attempts were being made to get at the definition of the term 'VALUE', many came across some of the phenomena that most people would regard as social problems: Crime, HIV transmission, religious bigotry, racism, unemployment, poverty, excess personal debt, etc. Theodorson and Theodorson also have been found similarly listing Drug Addiction, Juvenile Delinquency, Chronic, Unemployment and Mental Illness. However, if one tries to look at the global community, are not war, starvation and genocide, for example, social problems? Further, in addition to this, is it not a fact that what might be intolerable in one society may be quite acceptable in another? Then, the question is, 'How exactly the term VALUE is to be defined?'

Man is a social being. As such, for every man, "understanding of our fellow-beings is important. But, this understanding come out to be fruitful only when it is sustained by sympathetic feeling in joy and sorrow". Hence, a positive aspiration and effort for an ethical-moral configuration of our common life is of ever-riding importance. Without ethical culture, there is no solution to human problems. A man's ethical behaviour is, in fact, based effectively on sympathy, education and social ties and needs. But all this can be achieved only by the corresponding values because value is the prime-motivating force behind the individuals thought, emotion and action. Further, man has always aimed at the development of human personality. Of course, the weightage of any one aspect or certain qualities have been always shifting in different periods in all societies. And, it has always been the chief concern of education to inculcate the qualities of Head, Hand and Heart. However, wherever there has been a lack of integration in these aspects of personality, there has arisen a need to bring out a reform in Education-Criterion to evaluate the integrated personality. Thereafter, from his first experience man started becoming aware of how to feel with, how to sympathise, etc. Such feelings were found to be of worth, and, consequently, they have become a part of his total being. Then, there came a realisation to give a rethinking to the total effect of education on the development of personality and accordingly, 'Value-based Education' became the important need of the hour. The inculcation of values in schools was seriously thought of. Thus, once we understand that the term 'VALUE' is closely related with the aims of education, then, it is not difficult to define the term 'VALUE'.

WHAT IS A VALUE?

Human values have been employed in wo distinctively different ways in human discourse. It is often said that a person has a value or an object has a value. These two usages have been explicitly recognised by writers in various disciplines such as Charles Mortris in Philosophy, Brevster Smith in Psychology and Roibin Williams in Sociology.

If one wants to know the origin of the term 'VALUE', it may be stated very firmly that the term 'VALUE' comes from the Latin word 'VALERE' which means 'to be of worth'. Whereas, the concise Oxford Dictionary defines the term 'VALUE' as the 'worth, desirability or utility of a thing'.

In fact, it is difficult to define values, for they are as comprehensive in a nature as our human life. Somewhere, some other dictionary states that 'value is that which renders anything useful, worthy or estimable. It is price, worth or importance of a thing'.

Value is "a concept explicit of implicit, distinctive of an individual or characteristics of a group of those desirable traits which influence the selection from available modes and ends of action."

In fact, value is an abstract term which is commonly regarded as an economic conception. In the words of John Dewey, "Value means primarily, to price, to esteem, to appraise, to estimate. It means the act of cherishing something holding it clear and also, the act of passing judgement upon the nature and amount of its value as compared with something else."

According to Rokeach, "Value is an enduring belief, a specific mode of conduct or an end state of existence, along a continuum of relative importance."

Values are part and parcel of philosophy. Hence, aims of education are naturally concerned with values. All education is, in fact, very naturally value-oriented. Each educational goal, whether originating in a person, a family, a community, a school or an educational system, is believed to be good. 'Good' is intended to mean here 'avoidance of bad'. If possible objective, is not good, then there is no reason for pursuing. But again, the same question spurts out, and when the question 'what is a value?' spurts out, we know something of its religion, philosophy and ideology. The guiding social aims and beliefs which are regarded as the important aspects of a culture, then, the different aspects of culture are also 'valued' by the people; and the ideas lying behind which they think worthwhile, are called as VALUES!

A value is a preference as well as conception of the preferable. According to Kluckohn a value is a conception of the desirable and not something "merely desired".

Values are defined as something which are desirable and worthy of esteem for their own sake. Human values are defined as those values which help man to live in harmony with the world. Values that may be included in the general definition of human values are love, brotherhood, respect for others — including plants and animals — honesty, sincerity, truthfulness, non-violence, gratitude, tolerance, a sense of responsibility, cooperation, self-reliance, secularism and internationalism.

R. M. Maclever, in his "THE WEB OF GOVERNMENT" has used the term 'MYTH' where the term 'value' is used. According to him, myths are "value impregnated beliefs and notions that men hold, that they live by or live for." He says that every society is held together by a myth-system and "all social relations are mythborn and myth-sustained." According to Maclever, myths include "the most penetrating philosophies of life, the most profound intimations of religion...." Since myth is usually understood as a fictitious story or belief, Maclever has used this term differently, far from normal use. A. K. C. Ottaway in his book 'EDUCATION AND SOCIETY' has rightly observed by saying "A myth suggests a popular idea which is not in fact true and one hesitates to apply this term indiscriminately to the philosophies and religions of mankind". Hence, the use here of the word 'VALUES' stands for the idea men live for.

In the most elementary sense, value means whatever is actually liked, prized, desired or enjoyed by anyone at any time. It is the actual experience of enjoying desired object or activity. Hence, 'value is an existing realisation of desire'.

Even though, value has been said to be the experience of pleasure and joy; value experience are not under the direct control of reason.

In spite of the definitions quoted so far, one more definition still remains and it is of the eminent sociologist Prof. R. K. Mukerjee, who defines 'value' as follows —

"Values are socially approved desires and goals that are internalised through the process of conditioning, learning or socialisation and aspirations."

The sociologists are concerned with the questions like value-diversity, value-clashes, value-tensions, value-conflicts, social change, socialisation, innovations, modernisation and preferred futures. The legitimacy of the sociologists' involvement is based on the task of examining the social relations and processes as valuation phenomena.

According to Shaver, "Values are standards and principles of judging worth. They are a criteria by which we judge things — people, objects, actions, ideas and situations — to be good, worthwhile, desirable or on the other hand, worthless, despicable, undesirable or somewhere in between these two extremes".

The Shaver's definition consists of three elements:

(i) Values are concepts, not feelings.

(ii) Values exist in the mind independently of self-awareness or public affirmation.

(iii) Values are dimensional rather than absolute categories.

Truly speaking, making an attempt to define the term 'VALUE' is really a difficult task. Yet, we have, so far, come across many definitions given by the eminent people. And, we now get one more definition as given by Paker which reads as follows — "Value is the assuagement of desire". But Perry, interprets the term 'VALUE' in terms of 'interest' or 'object of interest', whereas R. M. Williams defines value as "mode of organising conduct" or "the principles that guide human action".

We have already seen that the term 'VALUE' stands for 'worth'. However, still more perfectly, it may be said that the term 'VALUE' stands for 'intrinsic worth'. Whatever is actually liked, prized, esteemed, desired, approved or enjoyed by any one, is valuable. A interdependent, accepted or consistent set of value is called 'Value-System'.

Education is capable of developing strong and abiding values. At all times, education has built on value-system, conducive to the development of physical, intellectual, moral and spiritual life. In activates the latent capacities of the individual enabling him or her to recognise 'truth', 'duty' and 'goodness'.

One may go on adding lines after lines and write pages after pages about 'VALUE'. But truly speaking, a full, detailed description of value and also value-education would entail a study in itself. There are corroborating findings by many researchers, and when we try to analyse and then study the entire description of such researchers, one may come to the conclusion that value is really a forceful tool for the cultivation of social good, and, values are the very essence of human life! It is that system which aspires the people for leading good life. With regards to this, it is better to quote a statement given by Radhakrishnan Commission which runs as follows:

"If we exclude spiritual training in our institutions, we would be untrue to our whole historical development".

— *Radhakrishnan Commission of 1948.*

NATURE OF VALUES

From the definitions of 'VALUE' that have been stated earlier, certain most important things regarding values are noted. These are —

1. Values are not feelings, but they are concepts.
2. Values are express feelings but they are more than feelings.
3. Values exist in the mind, and, are independent of Public affirmation.
4. Values are absolute but they are dimensional. That is, values are a criteria for judging the degree of goodness of badness, rightness or wrongness.
5. Values are concepts heavily weighted with emotions and influence the child's selection from variable modes, means and ends of action.
6. Values are primarily, ethical, social and subjective. Therefore, they are strong dispositions of human behaviour than concepts with less heavy emotional weightage.
7. Values are based on respect for human dignity. They assume that pesonal integrity is the nucleus around which ethical community and global stewardship resolve.
8. Values are the very essence of human life.
9. Values are essential for a fair and equitable community which reflects our respect as well as responsibility for the global environment.
10. Values are cross-cultural and are essential for the development of community and global citizenship.
11. Values are that in which people are interested.
12. Values are the things of worship.
13. Value is the product of feeling, set and action.
14. Values are the product of human spirit and not of intellect.
15. Values never change. It is only the perceptions of these that undergo changes as a result of ever-evolving human consciousness.

16. Values act as forceful tools for the cultivation of social good.
17. Values are caught through literature.
18. Value is a motivating force behind the individual's thought, emotion and action.
19. Values are integrated into personality and many times they act as barriers to the acceptance of new change or innovations.
20. Every value is reflected in a person's reactions.
21. Values influence every aspect of educational process.

Once again there is a temptation to quote Kothari Commission and Sri Prakasha Commission on Religions and Moral Instruction, which is stated as below —

"Every effort must be made therefore to teach students true moral values from the earliest stage of their educational life".

— *Sri Prakasha Committee on Religious and Moral Instruction*

Kothari Commission (1964-66) reads as follows —

"A serious defect in the school system is the absence of provision for education in social, moral and spiritual values".

CONCLUDING REMARKS

Concludingly, it may be said, then, that a value is what is desired or what is sought. Values may be operatioally conceived as those guiding principles of life which are conducive to one's physical, mental health and also to social welfare and adjustment that are in tune with one's culture. Values that reflect themselves in the expressions and experiences of the individuals in social institutions are both subjective and objective, human and divine. Such values are the criterion on the basis of which all immediate interests, desires and preferences are appraised. In fact, values do not have equal importance. Different authorities have assigned different importance to each of them. For example, some people have placed worship at the top of the list and health at the bottom. Yet, others have kept recreation above helath. However, the variations in the importance of values that are taken up as the criterion to recognise may remain the same.

Values are caught through literature. Codes and dogmas are confortable resting places to sustain the emotional needs of the adherent, but, in a fast changing world they tend to outline their credibity and usefulness. In a mobile world with vast cultural interactions, mere laws cannot foster a true understanding. It is in the reading of world literature that we get a better understanding of other human beings in particular and human values in general.

Human values are the product of human spirit and not of intellect. If human values are to be transmitted, they have to be first of all, intangible to the human heart.

4 KINDS OF VALUES

INTRODUCTION

Value-based approach to education is very significant and it is very essential for all of us to have a look at this issue very carefully. It is in the said connection, important to note that there are very few explicit references to values, and therefore, number of important questions begin to emerge:

- How many values are there?
- Which values are more important?
- Which values take secondary position?
- Could the entire values be modified so that we can include more specific references to values?
- Which particular values can be taken up as relevant for the learning areas?
- How, in fact, could teachers and schools more effectively integrate values into classroom practice and school life?

Such questions have provoked unending debate, but these questions have made us aware of the fact that because of the pluralistic and multicultural nature of our society, any agreement on values could be difficult to find. This is because, the number of values range from 3 to 83 (Reported and listed by NCERT). There exist various types of values among educators, sociologists and even among common public. Still further, it may be brought out to our readers that there exist different kinds of values — viz. there are personal values, community values, neighbouring values — or another classification may be Ultimate Values, Democratic Values, Educational Values — or still further, there are Values in relation to God, in relation to oneself, in relation to society etc. etc. or there may be values divided into subjective and objective, or there may be instrumental and intrinsic values or there are values that are used for valuing and others that are used to evaluate. Also, there are certain kinds of values named according to their specifications — for instance, there are aesthetic values in connection with arts, dancing, painting, music, dramatization, etc. Spiritual values concerning spirit as opposed to matter, divine matters and soul, moral values relating to ethics and social values concerning society and its well-being. Hence, it is necessary to have a detailed look into various kinds of values. Let us discuss all of them one by one.

First let us find out in detail about the three types of values mentioned earlier viz. — Ultimate Values, Democractic Values and Educational Values.

ULTIMATE VALUES

Value statements that identify the significance of certain ideas, experiences and activities to us, are the ultimate values. These go beyond mere statements of intellectual belief to the extent that they represent the beliefs that affect our decision on how to live. Human beings tend to rank their values in a rough order of priority, in accordance with ultimate beliefs about the world and their place in it. Religious traditions represent the most systematic attempts to explain our place in the world, and supply different accounts.

There are certain value statements about the Ultimate Values that represent the level of agreement achieved between several theistic religious traditions. The following aspects show or represent the ultimate values taken for granted from four different angles:

1. LIFE PERSPECTIVES: Here God is taken as the Creator and Self-revealer and about the religion is it said that religion arises from the human responses to God.

2. INDIVIDUAL: Each individual realises God given wholeness and is to encourage self-respect and learn from cultural traditions.

3. SOCIETY: Each individual recognises the human rights and is consistent with what we know to be the law of God — developing relationship in accordance with God's commandments.

4. NATURAL WORLD: Nature is appreciated as a gift of God and our relationship to nature is that of stewards, charged with managing it in trust for future generations.

DEMOCRACTIC VALUES

Democracy consists of a Society in which all people have equal rights to participate in the political process, while exercising the freedom to live as they choose, provided they do not infringe the right of others to do the same. Democracy, therefore, is a procedural notion, not an ultimate vision of living. For this reason, people with differing ultimate values may be prepared to accept a number of values whose practical justification is the maintenance of a viable democratic state and sustainable environment, thought they might have different ultimate reasons for being prepared to endorse those values. The following aspects show or represent the Democractic Values taken for granted from four different angles:

1. LIFE PERSPECTIVES: Here, search for knowledge, especially that which enhances the achievement of the other ends, is taken for value consideration. So too, right of all individuals to freedom to worship or not to worship is taken into consideration.

2. INVIDUAL: Here, the basic rights of all people regardless of differences to race, gender, ability and religious belief, is thought of and each inidividual is encouraged to contribute to the community services consistent with good citizenship.

3. SOCIETY: Responsibility is provided as a safety net for those in the society who lack the capacity through sickness, disability or unemployment, to sustain a viable lifestyle.

4. NATURAL WORLD: Nature is taken for conservation of the environment, and the need to continue to develop natural resources to sustain human life is taken into consideration.

EDUCATIONAL VALUES:

In addition to the values associated with common life with regards to Ultimate Values as well as Democractic Values, education draws on —

(*i*) Values intrinsic to the knowledge it seeks to impact, and

(*ii*) The ethics of providing instruction to human beings within the constraints of the classroom. The following aspects show or represent the Educational Values taken for granted from four different angles:

1. LIFE PERSPECTIVES: Encouragement is given to the students to explore the moral point of view and to develop a personal value system.

2. INDIVIDUAL: Every child has the right to access to available knowledge at an appropriate developmental level.

3. SOCIETY: Critical reflections are recognised on both the cultural heritage and the attitudes and values underlying current social trends. A social obligation to support research that promises to improve the quality of human life and to share the benefits as widely as possible is also noted.

4. NATURAL WORLD: There is a human drive to understand the realities of the world as being a valid quest for truth in its ultimate unity, and the aims of understanding of all the domains of human experiences — especially physical, intellectual, aesthetic, social, moral and spiritual is promoted.

Values, at the outset are not bifurcated as shown in the above manner alone, but values are, at the outset are divided into still many other ways. Let us now discuss about the Subjective and Objective types of values.

SUBJECTIVE (OR INTERNAL) VALUES

Some educators hold the view that educational values are internal and subjective. They are biological and psychological in origin. They satisfy the wants and desires of the student. They do not have any intrinsic or inherent worth of their own. Only the students or teacher 'value' them from his or her point of view and needs, instincts and emotions.

OBJECTIVE (OR EXTERNAL) VALUES

There are other educators who regard educational values as external and objective. They do not believe that they are just internal or private concern of the teacher of the student. The followers of this view believe that personal desire may be an important element of educational value, but they hold that values are independent of such desire.

Values are again divided into

(i) Instrumental and (ii) Intrinsic Values.

1. INSTRUMENTAL: The Instrumental Values are values which are judged good for something. That is, their values are dependent on the consequences or the outcomes.

2. INTRINSIC VALUES: On the other hand, Intrinsic Values are interest in the objects, not imposed or applied by outside agencies. They are judged good not for something else, but are good in and of themselves.

There are still another two types of values from an altogether different point of view to 'value'. Some values are used to value and others are utilised to evaluate. The same distinction is evident in the values "to prize and to appraise", "to esteem and to estimate". Similar difference also appears in "what is desired and what is desirable."

It is very significant to note then, that values have been variously classified. There is still one more type given by Shaver. Shaver has classified values as aesthetic, instrumental and moral. There are still others who have classified values as PERSONAL, COMMUNITY and NEIGHBOURLY VALUES. Let us have a look at these now.

PERSONAL VALUES

The values that are prescribed by the individual alone, irrespective of his or her social relationships, are termed as personal values — e.g. Dignity of Labour, Sensitivity, Cleanliness, Politeness, Honesty, etc. are Personal Values.

NEIGHBOURLY VALUES

Unlike personal values, the practice of neighbourly values necessitates the interaction of two or more persons. For instance, one can exhibit his or her patience with oneself, but this value is correctly actualised in the exercise of calmness and tranquillity with another person or persons.

COMMUNITY VALUES

The values that entail the complexities of wider interactions between groups of people are termed as community values. For instance, treating all in a friendly and loving manner can be practised by one individually with one's neighbours.

So far, we have seen various categories of values, yet, a three-tier hierarchy of values still remains to be discussed. These are OKAY values, NOKAY values and New values.

OKAY values are those values that can be acquired and transmitted. These are universal, eternal values such as Truth, Compassion, and these are also constitutional values like Secularism, Socialism etc. These have to be reinstated and given a new relevance and respect. NOKAY values are those values that can be consciously and habitually discarded. These are the beliefs and attitudes like 'vulgar consumerism', 'mindless defiance of authority' which are to be considered wrong and curbed resolutely. New Values are those values that can be created and adopted. These have emerged from the process of modernisation and urbanisation such as 'environment', 'preservation', 'value of time', 'punctuality', 'Public Hygiene' which can be acquired and fostered by teachers.

In fact, value experiences are not under the control of direct reason, but values are the product of feeling, set and action. It is here that we come across again another kind or type of values that are as follows, and these values have been classified into six categories as per the things in which a person is interested which are described as below —

1. THEORETICAL VALUES: Dominant interest in the discovery of truth.

2. ECONOMIC VALUES: A characteristic interest in all that is useful in terms of money, and that which is useful for the satisfaction of bona fide needs.

3. AESTHETIC VALUES: Places high ranking on beauty as an art.

4. SOCIAL VALUES: Highest love for the people. The social man prizes other persons as ends and is therefore himself kind, sympathetic and unselfish.

5. POLITICAL VALUES: Main interest is to gain prestige and power.

6. RELIGIOUS VALUES: The highest value for a religious man may be called unity and he seeks to comprehend the cosmos as a whole, to relate himself to its embracing totality.

CONCUDING REMARKS

Whatever manner one may classify the value, one significant thing to be noted that all values are operative as following levels —

- In relation to God
- In relation to oneself
- In relation to one's family
- In relation to one's school
- In relation to one's community and
- In relation to one's nation.

On the whole, values are desirable as well as favourable for the individual and the society for promoting individual and social development and well-being.

A value is what is desired or what is sought, and values of various kinds are named according to their specifications. It has been very rightly pointed out by M. R. RAMJI that —

"Values may be operationally conceived as those guiding principles of life which are conducive to one's physical and mental health as well as to social welfare and adjustment and which are in tune with one's culture".

How very true!

Values are related to life and in view of subdtlely values play a quiet game on the human sensibilities. The elements in the various types of kinds of values always sustains our interest, and each value that is pertaining to his or her interest is dear to the heart as one is more open to their influence!

Those of us who are both teachers and teacher educators, will readily acknowledge the frustrations of young adolescents. The ten most important values prescribed by Government of Maharashtra, affirm the need to equip students with the tools to examine world-views — both religious and non-religious, especially those dominant in their background and school community. It acknowledges the need of all persons for a sense of personal meaning, and encourages critical reflection on questions constituting the self in relation to the natural and social worlds. If affirms the tentative and limited nature of socially constructed knowledge, and the need to make students aware of this.

A focus on ciritical thinking, creative imagination and interpersonal and vocational skills would enhance those "basic skills" that comprise the current curriculum. It is time to bring into our schools a post-modern view of the knowledge and learning which might more appropriately prepare them for the 21st Century. The most important ten values prescribed by the Government of Maharashtra provide a starting point for this much needed reform of schooling.

Last but not the least, it may also be noted that values are unlimited, and values are interconnected too. To recognise and explore the significance of one value is to experience the unlimited treasure store of underlying and supporting values.

5

EDUCATION TODAY AND TOMORROW WITH SPECIAL REFERENCE TO VALUE EDUCATION

INTRODUCTION

No one can deny the fact that today education has continued to evolve diversity. It has extended its coverage since the dawn of human history. It has formed a continued bases for the development of human societies through the development of attitudes, values and capabilities, both of knowledge and skill.

Dr. S. Radhakrishnan has rightly said that education is there to help us find out what we are for in the world, and the three Rs of education should be replaced by three Hs, i.e., Head, Heart and Hands.

VALUES AND EDUCATION

Entire essence of life is found in value, nay, values are the essence of life. They are defined as morals, which build the character of human beings. In fact, values like kindness, love and tolerance have practised even animals and birds. Men of character build a disciplined community which provides the nation with political leadership, active and alert administrative personnel, wise parents, teachers full of enthusiasm and responsible citizens, who in turn develop a strong and progressive nation.

Education is the only instrument to bring about the desirable change in society. Education by its very nature is meant to achieve the function of making child the ultimate beneficiary. It has to provide vitality, vibrancy, strength and meaning to the learner's personality and purpose in life.

Education is a vital medium to imbile faster and perpetuate values in man. It activates the latent capacities of the individuals to recognise the truth, beauty and goodness. The hallmark of his personality are self-determination, self-realisation, self-integration, social adjustment, economic self-reliance and moral and social attitudes towards others. Value-Education, by training of mind and soul, gives the intellectuals wisdom and practical power, develops fearlessness of mind, strength of conscience and the integrity of purpose.

There is a nationwide realisation today that erosion of human values in our society is fast approaching a critical stage. A serious crisis of values is seen in human life. We have knowledge of science without the wisdom of soul. We have conquered space but lost control of our inner self. We have gained material prosperity but lost peace of mind! We have attained degrees without personal character and professional training without social and ethical omission.

Education at present, with its emphasis on consumerism and competition for achievement has sidelined its central concern for the full development of social, moral, aesthetic and spirtual side of human personality. Value-education which needs to be looked upon as an essential aspect for the overall qualitative improvement of education is being neglected to a great extent. The crisis today is not so much intellectual as spiritual. Unprecedented charges have overtaken us in recent times and knowledge, particularly scientific and technological knowledge, is today, burgeoning at an exponential pace which was not dreamt of some decades ago. The crux of the problem is that human spirit finds itself in a quandary because of its dismal failure to raise itself to take the bull by the horns. Bhagwan Satya Sai Baba has said — 'Today, selfishness has entrenched in the intellect. Compassion has dried up, Gratitude has waned. The scriptures are disregarded. Hypocrisy has become the hallmark of life. In the Kali age, these have become the qualifications of an educated person'. From these anguished words of Bhagwan Satya Sai Baba, the picture that presents itself is that of a great country like ours in a state of moral degeneration.

APPROACHES TO VALUE-EDUCATION

The development of values is not an easy job. There is no magic formula, technique or strategy for the inculcation and development of values. The very process of value-education is a very complicated task and its influenced by variety of hereditary and environment factors.

Generally, value-education programmes involve direct, indirect or incidental approches of value-development. Direct Approach refers to deliberate, systematic instruction in specially provided period in the school time-table. In most of Schools, value-education is imparted in this way. In this approach, the value to be inculcated and developed are explained, discussed and illustrated through stories, aneedotes, moral dilemmas, real life events.

Through Indirect Approach, value-education is imparted through regular subjects of the school curriculum and co-curricular activities. Whenever the value-inculcation and development are restored to in relation to a specific event that actually occurs in the school, is known as Incidental Approach of value-education. The example of this is the act of courage and bravery by a student.

Truly speaking, a well-known fact is that values are guides to human behaviour and that, school years are crucial for developing one's system of values. The individual grows and learns through experiences. Out of the experiences may come certain general guides to behaviour. These guides tend to give direction to life, and these are termed as values. These are two types of experiences — school experiences and out of school experiences. Both are equally important. But it is equally important to note that whatever the experiences are, we as teachers, have to structure them for the best possible results. There are three main approaches that are commonly known for value-oriented education. These are —

1. Critical Inquiry Approach (CIA)
2. Total Atmospheric Approach (TAA)
3. INTEGRATED CONCURRENT APPROACH (ICA)

Let us now try to discuss each of them separatey.

1. THE CRITICAL INQUIRY APPROACH

That type of education is ideal which begins with critical inquiry, and particularly for the clarification of values, it is essential children must be helped to discover what is right through constant critical inquiry and then harness their inherent energies for the pursuit of sound values. In fact, the dynamism of the student is to be taken as a starting point and basis for the process of value inquiry. Such a value inquiry is undertaken by the student with the help of the teacher. In such a process the student perceives that which is right and valuable. Soon he or she accepts the same and it is followed. According to Critical Inquiry Approach, there is no gap left between discovery and action.

In a Critical Inquiry Approach, more than the 'content', teaching of the reasoning skills is of crucial importance. A set of reasoning skills is to be furnished to the students, and then, they should be posed with a question — 'which am I to use in the real world?' For instance, a student is faced with a dilemma — either to speak the truth or tell lies. Now, if the student happens to speak the truth, then, the student also knows that on account of speaking the truth, someone will be put into trouble! Question is — should I speak the truth or tell lies? Such type of dilemmas are usually used for giving an opening to a new line of thought, to test the principle or to raise questions about a particular view point which is already taken for granted.

The Critical Inquiry Approach helps the students in clarifying the nature and consequences of the values and then to become thoroughly committed to their values. In fact, this is really a crucial aspect of any sound approach to value-education for becoming more aware of the values one has, so that one may evaluate them critically.

TECHNIQUES USED IN CIA

Out of the many techniques that are used in Critical Inquiry Approach, the following four are noted:

A. Media Approach

B. Simulation Model

C. Jurisprudential Inquiry Model and

D. Value Analysis Model

A. The Media Approach

An agency of communication is called 'media'; and, for conveying a message, all communication use media. The media is either oral i.e. verbal and written i.e. non-verbal. In these two different types of media we have newspapers, magazines, films, pictures, cartoons, posters, radio, television, cinema, video, internet extract from books, etc.

B. The Simulation Model

Simulation is controlled representation of reality. Simulation approach is a gaming approach. Here, the students are asked to participate (say dramatization or even role play) only the dimly imagining. It is that approach which involves the method of investigation along with the development of values and attitudes in pupils. Simulation helps to bridge a gap between theory and practice, by dwelling on experiential learning.

C. The Jurisprudential Inquiry Model

Regarding social values, there always exists in the society a conflict that is very natural. It is expected that, regarding certain controversial issues, the people should negotiate their differences very successfully by analysing the problem — For instance, "should there be mercy-killing or should there are be not?"

It is the Jurisprudential Inquiry Model that helps one to think systematically, and also helps one to rethink his or her position on important legal, ethical and social questions.

Jurisprudential Inquiry Model (JIM) consists of six phases. These six phases are divided into two parts — Analysis and Argumentation.

In the analysis of the JIM, we have following 3 phases:

1. Orientation to the case
2. Identifying the issues and
3. Taking positions

1. In the first phase of the analysis part of the JIM, the teacher introduces the case material and also reviews the facts.

2. In the second phase of the analysis part of the JIM, the studenrts synthesize the facts and then select only policy for discussion. Here they not only identify the value and value conflicts but also identify the spurting out questions therein.

3. In the third phase of the analysis part of JIM, the students articulate a position and state the basis of their position in terms of social values and also the consquences of their decision.

In the Argumentation part of JIM, we have following three phases:

1. Exploring the pattern of Argumentation

2. Qualifying the positions and

3. Testing factual assumption behind qualified positions.

1. In the first phase of the Argumentation part of JIM, students not only identify points of value violation but also clarify value conflict. After providing the desirable and undesirable consequences of the positions taken, the students also set value priorities.

2. In the second phase of the Argumentation part of JIM, students reason for their positions that they have stated and then by examining the similar situations, they qualify their positions.

3. In the third phase of the Arugmentation part of JIM, students determine the relevancy of factual assumptions and then examine the validity of predicted consequences.

D. THE VALUE ANALYSIS MODEL (VAM)

It is a fact that values often come into conflict with each other. Whenever there is restlessness and confusion in the minds of the individual, conflicts spurt out. Hence, it is of utmost importance to train our students to arrive at appropriate conclusion whenever the conflicting situations arise. This training can be given through Value Analysis Model, which is helpful to develop the reasoning power.

VAM consists of seven phases:

1. Presenting The Dilemma: This is presented through a situation (by narrating), or a film, or film strip, or even a set of pictures. The teacher must make sure that the dilemma is thoroughly understood by the class.
2. Clarification of Value Conflict: Here the teacher asks probing questions and then clarifies the conflict.
3. Asking For Conceivable Alternatives: Here all the possible alternatives are clarified through a brainstorming process.

4. Asking for Possible Consequences of Each Altenative: After having taken into consideration the alternatives, the consequences of those alternatives are discussed.
5. Asking for Evidences to Support the Likelihood of Each Consquence Occuring: Here, the students are asked to search for evidence, and this really encourages the students to search for data (reports, photographs, eye-witness accounts, etc.)
6. Asking for Evaluation of the Desirability of Likely Consequences: In this stage, the students are asked to consider whether they would want each consequences to happen or not. They can then be evaluatd from the moral, economic, educational, legal, social etc. points of view.
7. Determining the Best Alternative and Presenting Reasoning for the Same: In this last stage, the various alternatives are ranked in order of preference, and the most preferable is determined along with the reasons for their choice.

Concluding it may be said that the Value-Analysis Model is the effective way of training students to deal rationally with all types of ethical problems.

2. TOTAL ATMOSPHERIC APPROACH (TAA)

Another view on values is that knowledge of right and wrong and reasoning in values is not difficult to attain. Value education based on this concept involves the use activities, exercises and procedures in the entire school programme and habituate children in right mode of conduct, thus strengthening their character.

In the Total Atmospheric Approach, a planned attempt is made to influence entire atmosphere of the school. This approach really acts as the necessary intermediary and reflective stage in the teaching-learning process.

According to Total Atmospheric Approach, the following three are the major areas within the school system that are important for the value-inculcation:

1. The Curricular Programme
2. The Co-curricular Activities and
3. The Personal Example set by staff of the school.

1. The Curricular Programme emphasizes on the fact that the subject of language, Science, Mathematics and Social Sciences can be used for the integration of values with the school environment — for instance, a conscious efforts can be made to draw out values from languages to understand human nature. A respect for truth and conservation of the environment can be developed through the teaching of science. A value of mental discipline can be made known to student through the study of

mathematics and for the promotion of understanding the social environments, social sciences can be used to inculcate values.

2. The Co-curricular Activities are to be encouraged for that active participation which is skill based. For instance, active participation in games, sports etc. are to be encouraged as they help to develop body physique, active participation in debate, elocution, quizzes, etc. are to be encouraged as they help to develop the intellect and active participation in drama, music, etc. are to be encouraged as these help to develop emotions.

For inculcation of other social values like team work, cooperation, sensitivity to the needs of others, etc. can be inculcated by the daily school activities like assembly, excursion, picnics, celebrations of festivals etc.

3. Personal Examples of the teaching staff are the best to promote values like punctuality, neatness, cleanliness, sensitivity, etc. in the student. A teacher is himself or herself punctual, courteous, is having scientific temper, is clean and tidy, etc. can definitely inculcate in his or her pupils the said values by setting an example!

Thus, the school atmosphere, the personality and behaviour of teachers, the facilities that are provided in the school, etc. will have a large say in developing a proper sense of value among the student world.

CONCLUSION

Certain values are being caught by our pupils depending on the total atmosphere that is provided in the schools — viz — school assembly, celebrations of religious festivals of all religions, work experience, social service programmes etc. — all these do help in inculcating the values of mutual regard, honesty, discpline, social responsbility, etc. Unfortunately, however, not many schools make planned effort to inculcate the values with the kind of activities, experiences and atmosphere provided in schools.

INTEGRATED CONCURRENT APPROACH (ICA)

After considering the two main approaches — Critical Inquiry Approach and Total Atmospheric Approach — it is now essential to concentrate on The Integrated Cocurrent Approach (ICA). The Integrated Approach is one in which the problems or topics are the main focus of inquiry, experience and action in school atmosphere. Units of study are centred on topics of everyday school and out of school experience such as friendship, rewards and punishments, neighbourhood, disadvantaged class children at school, work and leisure and so on.

Children should be made to narrate their good and bad experiences and collect impressions about their school and then discuss the values of the school. The reasons for impositions of certain rules should also be made explicit.

The Integrated Concurrent Approach (ICA) requires appropriate planning. Also, there must be a good deal of freedom for the students to disagree, modify or respond differently for testing and practising the ideas.

Concludingly, it may be said then that it is urgent to make our education Value-oriented Education which must blossom human excellence. The students should be made to learn different ways to make their judicious use collectively rather than with selfish motives.

6

MANAGEMENT OF VALUES THROUGH EDUCATION

INTRODUCTION

Main objective of value eduation is to inculate the essential values depending upon the objectives, they may be individual, social and national values for example in India, Maharashtra State has adopted the following values to be inculcated among the student through eduation. They are namely sensitivity, punctuality, neatness, scientific attitude, dignity of labour, sportsmanship, equality, brotherhood, patriotism, secularism, cooperation, tolerace, respect for elder, non-violence, national integrity, universal brotherhood.

An education system interlinked with our cultural heritage on one hand and economic and scientific, development on the other is only viable medium to take us successfully ahead towards 21st century. It is universal outlook that leads to the banishment of all evil influences may they be superstitions, hatreds or intolerance. World is becoming one, we are heading towards estabishment of a global civilisation an we contemplate of one government in future. When the differences of east and west would perish and values of like would be universalized.

According to John Dewey "Value primarily means to prize, to esteem, to apprise, to estimate, it means the act of cherishing somethings, holding it dear and also act of passing judgement upon the nature and amounts of values as compared with something else". Values are the part and parcel of the philosophy of the nation and its eduational system. Values are guiding principles of life, which are conductive to ones physical, social and mental health. Inculcation of desirable values is felt necessary through the education and for this purpose teachers, the educational institutions and society in general should be prepared.

It has been observed that there is an erosion of social and moral values of system. The Indian psyche is deeply embedded in spiritual value system drawn from thousands of years of common cultural heritage and educational system devoid of cultural values is not hollow in content but unsuitable as well. The values of culture and that of science are to be integrated proportionatley in such a way that culture will act as a catalyst to sharpen the scientific temperament of nation's youth. The educational systm should ensure aesthetic and qualitative life to its citizen besides achieving the economic and scientific targets. The invasion of electronic media in our country has further increased the importance of inculcating and presenting the cultural values in our society.

IMPORTANCE OF VALUE EDUCATION

In the existing educational system lays greater emphasis on individualism, competition, verbal fluency or linguistic ability and mere acquisition of information is given, this is just not sufficient and great emphasis will have to be given on the value education. Since it is the time to forge a reform civilizational coherence with broadly acceptable national cultural identity where social values and development can be naturally reinforcing.

The cultural values need to be identified for standard curricula all over the country. The value education should be imparted compulsority up to the high school level. Evaluation of value education should be routine one and it should be based upon the daily observations of student by teachers and peers and should be monitored by administrator properly and also by the parents.

In value education man is the object and it is said moral is caught and not taught and therefore the person inculcating moral values must be of very high moral standard. In other words the teachers who imparts these values must be selected in such a way that he should be reservoir of these values and capacity to transform them among the student with active participation and maintenance of good environment and also all the teachers should be in a position to suggest new projects and at the same time they should be in touch with the parents with their wholehearted support for inculcating such values.

Since July 1997 Maharashtra Government has introduced *'Paripath'* for this purpose in all schools.

It was observed that in spite of the efforts made by educationists, administrators and their implementators with the help of teachers the expectd results were not visualized.

The reasons behind not getting expected results and deterioration of these values following three aspects are responsible.

These are —

(1) Educational Institutions, (2) Society, (3) Administration.

All these factors are involved in the deteriorations of the values.

It goes without saying that to avoid the deteriorations efforts have to be made at all the three levels and inevitably teacher plays an important role in this regard. It is essential to always have the teachers of high esteem and moral. The self-respect of the teachers should be supported strongly by the society. Then no doubt it is possible to inculcate these values effectively as per expectations.

Since last two years in Maharashtra efforts are being made at all levels to inculcate these values. Maharashtra Government has introduced *paripath* since last two years in all schools. *Paripath* is morning prayer, in the beginning of school day which consist of national anthem, pledge, devotional songs, moral stories, good though, news, maun.

(A)1. All the teachers were of the view that *paripath* is essential.

2. Impact of moral stories is more effective.

3. Positive change in the behaviour of the student is observed.

(B) In another study undertaken it is observed that co-curricular activities which are necessary for inculcation of values are arranged in most of schools but rarely arranged in colleges and at the university level.

(C) In an another survey based upon the study of value education through co-curricular activities in Jalna district and on the basis of findings of this survey following recommendations are made.

1. Cultural education must be included as a component.
2. The teacher trainees should be cultural resource and should have a proper background of history, culture and artistic heritage of that area.
3. A networking of insitution involved in such activities is essential to maintain high standard of training such as CCRT, NCERT, SCERT.
4. As moral education is introduced in the first period in the time-table, grade should be given for the assessment of value education.

To achieve the expected goal it becomes highly essential to concentrate on important aspects namely the teachers, the administrators and the society.

SELECTION OF TEACHER AS A RESOURCE PERSON

He must be intellegent, resourceful and for that purpose efforts must be made to attract good persons from society to make carrier in this field and should shoulder the historical responsibility of building the nation.

Selection board is equally important and should select right person without any prejudices and should see that only right person will enter in this noble profession. A wrong teacher will spoil the class but wrong teaching agency spoils the nation.

We suggest following activities for effective management of the value education which are as given below:

1. *Paripath* is a regular activity of school, D.Ed. College, in the B.Ed. College and Junior and Senior Colleges it should be a regular activity.
2. Follow up activities should be conducted of *paripath,* some activities based on *paripath* should be organised.
3. Renowned persons, ideal teacher's contribution may be taken.
4. Through textbooks, especially of first languages, teaching should be done, keeping in view, what values will be inculcated through each lesson.
5. Media should disseminate non-formal education interestingly, literature, serials, movies should not encourage false belief, sex, violence.

For effective management of value education we suggest following recommendations:

1. Student should be rewarded for good habits and good deeds in assembly which will inspire other student.
2. Value education should be imparted compulsorily up to the high school level. Evaluation of value education should be routine one. It should be based on daily observation of the student by teachers and peers.
3. Non-formal programmes like educational visits, exchange of resource material, mobile exhibitions, regional seminars, visits to cultural and national monuments and museums needs to be emphasised.
4. All the teachers in the school should be regarded at teachers of value education and all the subjects including physical education can be used for inculcation of right values.
5. There should be formation of courses both at the secondary level and at university level aiming at giving the children basic knowledge about media, its people and cultural tradition.
6. Exchange of programmes amongst various states, countries, studying each other's cultures and literacy works should be taken up to develop a spirit of kindship and common value system.
7. The curriculum should be related to national integration, social justice, productivity, modernisation of the society and cultivation of moral and social values.

8. Co-curricular activities have physical, ethical, aesthetic, recreational, psychological, academic, social, cultural, disciplinary values for that proper selection of activities is an important part of organisation.
9. Co-curricular activities which are necessary for inculcation of values should be arranged rigorously.
10. A networking of institutions like CCRT, NCERT, SCERT is necessary to set high standards for training and strenthening of these institutions is equally important.
11. For the all round development of students the provision of special teachers for subjects like physical education, vocation, music, dance is to be made.
12. Fine arts, music, creative writing, puppetry and theatre are to be given due place in the curriculum right from the school to university level.
13. A postgraduate course in comparative religion may be instituted.
14. A fairly long period of social service should be introduced by all schools and universities.
15. Planned *paripath* should be a regular feature, followed by execution and evaluation.
16. Student should maintain a diary of daily activity and teacher should check it.

The school assembly, *paripath,* the curricular and co-curricular activities, the celebrations of religious festivals of all religious, work experience, team games and sports, subject clubs, social service programmes all these can help in inculcating the values of co-operation, discipline and social responsibility.

This value education should not be only for the children who are in the school but also for those who are outside it. Even parents, nonliterates, neoliterates should be involved in the project. In fact, the whole society has to be involved in the process of value oriented education.

Value education through literacy campaign continuing education centres have been started functioning in the country. *Paripath* should be arranged at the centre. Neoliterate knows many moral stores, there should be exchange of thoughts, experiences. Through moral stories, street plays, concepts of reading, writing and numeracy can be introduced in literacy classes as well. Reading culture should be developed in neoliterate also.

Moral education should be provided both by direct and indirect methods, by suggestions as well as by discussion and teaching.

A serious defect in the curriculum is the absence of provision for educaton in social, moral and spiritual values. In fact, the whole society has to be involved in the programmes of value oriented education. The root cause of today's unrest in the society is deterioration of values. There is a disparity in the ideal situation and present situation in the society. Society is devoid of devotion and emotion, it is through management, values can be inculcated and restored support and strengthening of values is the need of hour.

There has been a rapid erosion of ethical and moral values in Indian society after independence. As value education means positive efforts for bringing about asenthesis of physical, intellectual, emotional, aesthetic, moral and spiritual values in human beings so the present focus should be revival of values in education.

7

VALUE EDUCATION AND NEED FOR ITS INCULCATION

INTRODUCTION

The social, cultural and technical changes of recent times have brought about a change in the value system of our society. People of different strata of the society differs in their views and priorities, and as a result, there is no definite value-system to guide the life pattern of people. In fact, many are on the lookout for values that make life very meaningful as well as purposeful. But there is a gaping discrepancy between what one says and what one does. The patents offer one set of, value, school projects a different set of values, religion proposes yet another set of moralisation. The modern communication media offers in very attractive ways with all sort of stimuli and inputs about what to believe, how to behave, what type of lifestyle to adopt, etc. The peer group influence, ideologies of the political leaders, film stars, sports figures, each is adding to nothing but to the confusion of the confused mind, pose a dilemma to our youngsters today! Further, there is a lot of discrepancy in what one says and what one does. This is one of the reasons why students are losing respect for elders and teachers. We, as teachers, have therefore, to try to put ourselves in their shoes. We need to blame ourselves for value-degradation and not any system or institution. Hence, in such existing stage of confusion and conflict, it is the teachers to help our students to develop their own values-system. It is this fact, which has necessitated the teachers to use very many teaching strategies and facilitate the process of value-development and value-clarfication. The social, political and religious values legitimately conflict with one another. When there is a value-conflict three types of people are seen. The first type will withdraw and show a non-interfering attitude. The second type will conform and let others decide for them what to believe and do. The third type will fight the confusion trying to strike anything that troubles them. But, none of the three approaches will resolve the value-conflict. What is required is thinking as well as reasoning. One should be able to ask. "Do I know what I value?" "Are my actions consistent with what I think, feel and believe?" "Which values do I uphold and will publicly affirm?" Thus, it has become a challenge to a modern teacher to find out the way of making value-education effective and interesting to the wisdsom of pupils. Basically, everyone today, feels an inner urge for a sound value-system.

In the above said context, one can boldly say that our traditional education has failed to clarify values. It has helped us to decide when an action is right and when it is wrong. We say that our younger generation is going astray or their values are not those accepted by the society. The reason for it is that our system of education has not taught our children the art of making constant value-decisions. Students know only such set of values which happens to be right in the experience of a national hero, a social reformer or a religious leader. Values are neither caught nor learnt through imitation, they are developed through reasoning. The age of "Do as I say" or "should and should not" has gone. The rule of do's and don'ts will work only when there is a single set of desirable values in society. Students should be helped to develop a set of values which they think is right. As Sidney Simon (1974) has rightly said — 'values should not be based on external forces such as the power of propaganda, peer pressure or unthinking submission to authority'.

Say, somewhat sixty years ago, the question papers of our universities carried the name of paper setters. None in those days concerned himself or herself with trying to find out where the papers were printed. If the results happened to be strict, it was felt that the preparation was inadequate, and the standard maintained by the concerned universities were relatively high. All this seems incredible today where there is leakage in some place or other, when mass copying, boycott of the examination hall, no longer is shocking to us! We are all, in fact, astonishingly familiar with all such facts, over the years! It is almost forgotten today that we have a moral responsibility to provide the foundation for students moral development along with physical, intellectual and social development.

Thus, within the course of a generation and a little more, our sense of values and within it our capacity to adjust have undergone a remarkable change. Why has this happened? Why does the conscience pick up sharply no longer? Why has our sense and understanding of values progressively undergone a sort of devaluation? It is not merely the sacrd precincts of learning that have been polluted, other areas perhaps not so sacrosanct, have also suffered from similar invasions from the rank of corruption and dishonesty. In other words, there has been in many places a crisis of values.

Since very ancient times educational systems have served as a supreme agency of inculcating the values and norms of society in their members. In this sense, the role of schools, throughout has remained important. It is an unopposed and fully agreed fact that the main function of education is to promote a balanced development of physical, mental, social, moral and spiritual aspects of the students in order to produce balanced citizens who strive to promote social welfare and progress.

Education in the context of social change is not only to impact information and to teach skills to the students but also to inculcate the values of humanism, democracy, socialism, secularism and national integration. This is necessary for the realisation of our national objectives of building a democractic attitude that is based on equality, social justice, frateternity and freedom.

Several educationists in India as well as abroad have stressed the importance of promoting values through eduation. Radhakrishnan Commission, Kothari Commission and even the National Policy on Education, have brought to focus the need for re-adjustment in the curriculum in order to make education a forceful tool for the cultivation of values.

Value-inculcation or need to inculcate values is felt very much, therefore, because the values have suddenly disappeared form the school premises! Question is — "Have they disappeared suddenly?" Like slow-poisoning, it is only after death the doctor diagnoses the malady. So too, before disappearing from our school premises, values have disappeared from our homes too which were once the best schools where children learned their first lessons in values. Today, we live in a world where falsehood succeeds, corruption prospers and nepotism works, where that situation prevails in which "virtue itself of vice must pardon beg" as Shakespeare puts it. These are the values the young generation imbibe and inhale today. In fact, crisis of values is pervasive in schools, in colleges, in universities, amongst teachers as well, and is seen as the most dangerous development. It is, therefore, being urged that the process of education should be reoriented and young children should be made to realise that exploitation, insecurity and violence cannot be contained nor can an organised society be sustained without adhering to enforcing some norms of social, political and economic behaviour.

So too, it may be said that today's teacher is no longer an influential heir to imitate and emulate for the young generation. The exposure of the young to the teacher is marginal and ineffectual in comparison with the multitudinous stimuli around them.

WHAT IS VALUE-EDUCATION?

The very purpose and main function of education is the development of an all round and well-balanced personality of the students, and also to develop all dimensions of the human intellect so that our children can help make our nation more democratic, cohesive, socially responsible, culturally rich and intellectually competitive nation. But, nowadays, more emphasis is unduly laid on knowledge-based and information-oriented education which takes care of only the intellectual development of the child. Consequently, the other aspect of their personality like physical, emotional, social and spiritual are not properly developed in providing for the growth of attitudes, habits, values, skills and interests among the pupils. It is here that we talk in terms of value-education. A complete description of what value-education is, could entail a study in itself. There are corroborating findings, by many researchers. After analysing and studying the descriptions (about value-education) of such researchers the definition of value-education may be started as follows:

Value-education is a many sided endeavour and in an activity during which young people are assisted by adults or older people in schools, family homes, clubs and religious and other organisations, to make explicit those underlying their own attitudes, to assess the effectiveness of therse values for their own and others long term well-being and to reflect on and acquire other values which are more effective for long term well-being. Value-education, is thus concerned to make morality a living concern for students. Hence, what is needed is value-education. Despite many educators and educationists description regarding value-education, it cannot be denied that continuing research will continue to making the description of value-education more adequate.

According to C. V. Good — "Value-education is the aggregate of all the process by means of which a person develops abilities, attitudes and other forms of behaviour of the positive values in the society in which he lives.'

OBJECTIVES OF VALUE-EDUCATION

Traditionally the objectives of value-education were based on religion and philosophy. There was no secular value-education; but in today's modern world, this has been taken as very much essential. Accordingly, the objectives for value-education may be taken up as follows:

- Full development of child's personality in its physical, mental, emotional and spiritual aspects.
- Inculcation of good manners and of responsible and cooperative citizenship.
- Developing respect for the dignity of individual and society.
- Inculcation of a spirit of patriotism and national integration.
- Developing a democractic way of thinking and living.
- Developing tolerance towards and understanding of different religious faiths.
- Developing sense of brotherhood at social, national and international levels.
- Helping pupils to have faith in themselves and in some supernatual power that is supposed to control this universe and human life.

- Enabling pupils to make decisions on the basis of sound moral principles
- Evolving the evaluation criteria on value-education.
- Suggesting measures for better utilisation of value-education.
- Finding out the interests of pupils in relation to different aspects and activities of value-education.
- Clarifying the meaning and concept of value-education.

NEED FOR THE INCULCATION OF VALUE EDUCATION

Again and again, like a boomerang, the question that bursts out is "where have the values gone?' While making an attempt for answering this question, one notices a conscious and conspicuous shifts in the latter-day educational philosophy from a cognitive to kinetic development of the pupil. A wide range of values of moral, aesthetic and social nature that have evolved during the marathon march of the human civilisation is posing before us a crisis of priorities: which of these values is to be cultivated and what is the appropriate stage of doing so? Hence, the issue becomes all the more jumbled when it comes to fixing up of the responsibilities: who is to inculcate values? — parents, leaders, the affluent, the business tycoons, thinkers, artists, teachers? The easy and obvious answer is — "the teacher is the prime inculcator of values because the young are under his or her formal care".

Whatever may be the answer! Really speaking, it is not enough just to know about values, because values have to be practised. Our country is undergoing radical, social changes. So, the students who are the future citizens of tomorrow have to be oriented to respond to and adjust with these social changes satisfactorily by equipping them with desirable skills and values. The Modern India has committed to the guiding principles of socialism, secularism, democracy, national integration and so on. These guiding principles should be emphasised in the educational system and suitable values are to be included in the students for promoting equality, social justice, national cohesion and democractic citizenship. With these aims in view, radical reforms in the present lop-sided education are to be introduced and all attempts need to be made for developing well-integrated personalities for our individuals. Hence, the need for inculcating desirable values. India is known for its rich cultural and spiritual heritage, and the need for a value-system through education has been felt and recognised through centuries. Value system play an important role in any decision making process. In fact, every human action is the reflection of personal and social values.

Modern age of science and technology has created many evils. Violence, immorality, egoism, self-centredness, frustration are rampant everywhere. The world has already experienced the horrors of modern wars during WORLD WAR I and II. It has been the victim of passions and evils like violence, jealousy, national superiority and arrogance. That is why, in spite of wonderful, scientific achievements the world is a place of violence, gloom and unease. In the midst of material prosperity, a large section of humanity is under the grip of immorality, poverty and corruption. Thus, man has been the monarch of entire world. Now, such unsatisfactory situations have arisen due to crises of values. Hence, inculcation of desirable values in the student is felt essential to find out the answers to such questions as —

- What exactly is the wrong thing that is existing in today's entire educational system?
- How can international harmony and peace be promoted?
- How can social justice and also fellow-feeling be ensured in the modern world?
- Which things can be considered to be the most important causes for the outburst of crises that is seen or witnessed by all of us today?
- How can mankind carve out for itself a preferred future of peace and prosperity? etc. etc.

The Kothari Commission has very rightly observed "the expanding knowledge and growing power which is places at the disposal of modern society must, therefore, be combined with the strengthening and deepening of the sense of social responsibility and a keener appreciation of moral and spiritual values".

Now, looking at today's situation which is developing very fast, it is equally important for us to give a proper value-orientation to our educational system. Hence, after India gained Independence, continued attempts have been made for inculcation of right values in the students at different stages of education. Accordingly, the National Conference On Minimum Curriculum Standards for primary stage organised by NCERT (National Council For Educational Research and Training) in July 1970, emphasised the importance of inculcating in the students moral and spiritual values which form a part of our culture viz., honesty, kindness, charity, tolerance, courtesy, sympathy and compassion. The National Seminar on Primary and Work-oriented Education organised by NCERT in November, 1976, in the context of International Education Year recognised the relevance and importance of the Gandhian Values in reforming education. The Seminar, therefore, recommended the following Gandhian Values for inculcation at the Primary Stage —

1. Dignity on manual labour
2. Sense of social awareness and responsibility
3. Respect for other's religion
4. Fearlessness

5. Truthfulness
6. Non-Violence
7. Purity
8. Service and
9. Peacefullness

Dr. M. T. Ramji, in his book entitled as 'VALUE ORIENTED SCHOOL EDUCATION' has mentioned that in the context of modern India which is moving towards industrialisation and technology, we need education that is based on spiritual, moral and social values. According to him, the important spiritual, moral and social values which form part of the Indian Cultural Heritage are —

- Courage
- Truth
- Universal love
- Respect for all religions
- Dignity of manual work
- Service
- Purity
- Courtesy
- Peace and
- Joy

All these values are to be taught in Primary and Secondary Schools and it is imperative on the part of the teachers as well as teacher eduators to understand the school situation and also the potentialities of school activities in promoting the values in schools.

In a paper entitled — "EDUCATION IN THE FIFTH YEAR PLAN, 1974-79", brought out by the Ministry of Education and Social Welfare, Government of India, it is pointed out — 'Perhaps, the most significant need of hour is to transform the educational system with a view to cultivating the basic values of humanism, democracy, socialism and secularism....'

It is in the above quoted context, it may be stated firmly that the teachers, teacher-educators and administrators should try their best to promote value-oriented education in schools. Hence, it is essential to generate adequate awareness among the people through mass media as well as different types of school organisations. The schools can definitely play an important role in inculcating desirable values in the pupils through effective organisation of different, curricular and co-curricular programmes. Now, such a task must necessarily be the joint responsibility that is to be shouldered by all teachers and not just the assigned duty of one or two teachers.

Such "a growing concern over the erosion of essentials and an increasing cynicism in the society has brought to focus the need for readjustments in the curriculum in order to make the system of education a forefull tool for cultivation of social and moral values". (National Policy On Education, Government of India, 1986, pp. 21).

According to Burtrand Russel, "Broadly speaking, we are in the middle of a race between human skills as to means and human folly as to ends. The human race has survived owing to ignorance and incompetence, but given knowledge and competence combined with fully, there can be no certainty of survival. Knowledges is power for evil as much as for good. It follows that, unless men increase in wisdom as much as in knowledge, increase of knowledge will be increase of sorrow."

Love, compassion, sympathetic joy and even mindedness have obviously an unbalanced scope like wisdom and require a long, strenuous training and dedication of creative imagination and intuition. Such training in the East has been both emotional and intellectual. In the West, little attention has been paid to the cultivation and training of moral feeling, imagination and intuition (Renue Geenon Crisis of Modern World - p. 32).

In countries where there was but one official religion, the church, temple or mosque could provide the necessary authority to impose a common moral code on schools. But in most countries there are number of religions and cultures which, from time to time may have come into conflict. To assume peace and national unity, mostly countries have established secular public education system. Our population during the Post-Independence period has increased in terms of culture and religion; slowly we are beginning to see the richness and diversity of cultures, which is an asset to our nation, and to understand that diversity is valuable in its own right. Thus, we see on the one hand in the history of education the demand for an education which aims at developing social cohesion and respect for common values, but on the other, an education that is respectful of the dignity of every individual and every cultural identity. But the question is — "Can education promote unity in diversity, and if so, how?"

And — Mahatma Gandhi, long ago has answered — "I do not want my house to be walled in on all sides and my windows to be stuffed. I want the culture of all the lands to be blown about my house as freely as possible. But I refuse to be blown off my feet by any". Gandhiji remained an inspiration to all who wanted to support a vision of unity. He had understood the value of cultural diversity.

Today, we all are living such a society where we find anxiety-sticken parents, frustrated jobless degree holders, teachers strikes, dowry deaths, attraction of students towards private coaching classes, inability of our teachers to keep control over the overcrowded classes, etc. etc. On account of the said circumstances, there is very much a strongly felt need to develop value-education policies and programmes which will seek to eliminate all types of discriminaton in education. For this a planned action will be such where rights of minorities will be taken care of, where intellectual understanding will be promoted, where there will be tolerance for other religions. It is better to state in one sentence that we need to place the melting pot model by a mosaic, rich in diversity but nonetheless having a clear unifying pattern based on 'global ethics'.

The matter that has been discussed so far, brings out adequately the need for value education which will lead to the regeration of values that have been lost in the process of search of knowledge, power and material progress during this century and preceding ones. It is because of this, it seems, Kothari Commission has rightly stressed — "A National System Of Education that is related to life, needs and aspirations of the people cannot afford to ignore this purposeful force — viz. VALUE".

The National Policy On Education of 1986 has very strongly recommended the need for value-education due to the following reasons —

- Tremendous advance in science and technology has resulted in a complete change in the lifestyle of the people.
- Science and technology is being used to produce weapons of mass destruction endangering the very existence of the human race instead of using it for the betterment of human life.
- Erosion of traditional values.
- Life in the future is going to be faster and more complex. The student of today have to face such moral situations in future, in which, instead of depending on others, they may be required to take their own decision.
- The present youth has special problems. It has started to question the conduct of elders — especially political leaders. They do not see the relevance of the values preached.

The above discussion stresses again and again the importance of the need of value-education. Value-education involves exposing students to a whole series of values in their complete totality. I helps to bring about an improvement in the child's thoughts, ideas attitudes, interests, emotions, sentiments, personality and character. Really speaking, value-education influences all aspects of a person's growth and development. Thus, value-education consequently, is an integral part of education which cannot be separated from the educational process. Value-education has to be placed, therefore, at the centre of the educational endeavour. Schools should be induced to create a climate of values which should run various activities and would be conducive to the promotion of values among students, teachers, parents and educational administrators. Programmes of value-education should incorporate values of integral personality in all its dimensions — physical, vital, intellectual, aesthetic, ethical and spiritual.

The question now jumps up — How exactly the implementation of such value-education could be done in schools and what are the various activities to be undertaken in different classes? The process of valuing is what we go through when we make judgement about things, events and people that we encounter in our day-to-day life. Therefore, once again the question 'How should we impart values through education?' comes to our mind and once again, as an answer to this question, we will have to concentrate on an altogether different chapter.

THE EMERGENCY OF VALUE EDUCATION IN THE INSTITUTES OF HIGHER LEARNING

8

INTRODUCTION

Values hold a unique inherited strength for which our country India stands at the most prominent place admist developing and developed countries of the world. This is the time when reawakening is taking place with a realisation that values which formed an integral part of India's rich heritage has been receding into the dark. Every need is felt to revive the most significant value patterns that are indispensable part of our lives. The attractions of the Western world have been changing the ideologies of our children. They are not aware of the richness of inherited traditions of our country, which stand on the strong foundations of values our ancestral possessed. The global influences, *misinterpretd most of the time* have been affecting our society vis a vis education system. While looking into this emerging scenario, one can stipulate that the time has arrived when one needs to insist on right education that imparts right values to our young generation. The wave can take a stride from primary to secondary and senior secondary stages of education reaching the greater heights at the institutes for higher learning when wisdom becomes more enduring and is carried throughout life. This revival in the thoughts mainly came from Delors Commission (1996) which recognises the need for universities to take up responsibility for development of the society as a whole Universities and other institutes of higher learning have been accepted as one of the thriving forces for passing on the accumulated experience an culture where primarily all the traditional functions are extended to advancement and transmission of knowledge i.e., research, innovation, teaching and training and continuing education. The transition does however communicate the importance of orientation of value education to our future generation to drive them towards acceptable standards naturally through the process of education.

VALUE EDUCATION: A VARIETY IN CONCEPT

Sri Aurobindo while emphasizing upon the true basis of education as the study of the human mind stresses upon the need to inculcate right values, right from infancy to adulthood. He emphasizes on three principles of education *"Nothing can be taught -------- the teacher is a helper and a guide. His business is to suggest and not impose ...... And mind has to the far from that which is to that which shall be"*. Sri Aurobindo has been emphasizing on two prime functions of higher education: *knowledge of thing and knowledge of men* (human right action, nature, creations — (History, Philosophy, Art, Mathematics and now liberal to include modicum of science). He advocated that to make liberal and original knowledge, it is necessary to make available sound culture where a general desire as a motive for education exists. It is also largely accompanied with the earlier feeling that knowledge is necessary to keep up one's position in society and to succeed is certain lucrative or respectable profession.It is here that higher education can play a facilitating role in helping students to cultivate the best, and make the best use of it in the years to come.

In the Meet for Vice-Chancellors on value orientation education (1984), the then Governor of Rajasthan, Shri O. P. Mehr observed "We seem to completely ignore the eternal and universal values. The world value as understood in the context of educational philosophy refers to those desirable ideals and goals that are intrinsic in themselves and which when achieved or attempted evoke a deep sense of fulfilment". In the present times, with the progress of materialistic society, our stress is so much on standards of living and not on standards of life. In this changing scenario, the very concept and interpretation to the term 'Value' is undergoing a change. The eternal values of truth, love, happiness, compassion and character are itself losing the meanings for which it stood during ancient prosperous times. This gives the impression that now is the time when we need to recognise the importance of meaning of such values and create situations, which bring back the richness of our heritage that has receded into the dark. As Swami Vivekanand comments, "The idea of all education, all training should be man-making. Education is not the amount of information that is put into your brain and runs right there, undigested, all your life. We must have life-building, man-making, character-making assimilation of ideas." In the words of Sri Satya Sai Baba, *"Education is for man-making, nation building and promotion of peaceful world order"*. The man-making includes a five-fold aspects of personality growth which are at the mental, physical, emotional, psychic and spiritual level; and include the human values of truth, righteous conduct, peace, love and non-violence.

"We are in the midst of an all pervaisve process of social Westernisation that is accelerated by the rapid pace of industrialisation and mechanisation resulting in the wholesale liquidation of the humane and universal values of our ancient civilisation." Thus, the first objective of higher education should be to turn out integrated personalities with noble ideals. The university campus should stress on the importance of individual self-fulfilment but not self-indulgence. Group cohesiveness but not group jingoism and work and achievement but not power and acquisitiveness for their own sake. The second function of education is to enrich the character. What we need today more than anything else is moral leadership that rests on the strong foundation of courage, intellectual integrity and a sense of values inculcated.

ORIENTATION OF VALUE EDUCATION IN THE HIGHER EDUCATION SET UP: SOME SIGNALS

Since our independence, there has been an enoromous quantitative expansion in the number of schools, colleges and universities, but with well-known erosion in the quality of education. It might have developed the intellectual abilities and technical skills but the humane and the emotional aspects based upon the good practices for better onward journey has been a missing link. This certainly calls for an effective designing, programming and implementation of value education characteristics entwined into the learning processes taking place in the college and university campus. The execution of value orientation in higher education requires a well chalked out planned actions and strategies, few of which could be discussed as follows:

➤ *Organisational Arrangements for Planning and Monitoring*

In the light of a number of recommendations flowing from different directions, the most accepted one is to appoint a National Commission, that is expected to convene national debates, seminars and symposiums, constituting working groups, to prepare a plan of action in the university or school, mobilize funds from government and manage monitoring groups to carry out follow up activities NIEPA has brought out a publication on "Integral Education: A mission to integrate values into Education" an experiment by SSI Institute of Higher Learning Board guidelines from such universities seem to be a useful proposition. One can always draw, tailor and translate practices and policies along with the courses offered in these universities.

Intertuining of Value Education in Co-curricular Activities: Formal or Informal, Direct or Indirect Courses

While the direct courses can be designed in detail by the concerned university, the indirect courses can also find place in normal activities of the university campus and the colleges. Tagore and Gandhi have laid great stress on the creation of conductive atmosphere in the campus. There is every need to link teaching of every subject with underlying objective of value education in an integrated manner with sensitization and awareness created throughout the process of learning. These could be adapted from the best practices from other countries as well. Some of the popular practices may be followed like direct instructions, special programme of study discussions, talks and speeches by eminent scholars, daily assembly, collective workshops, extra-curricular activities including yoga, sports and games, formation and discussion of classroom rules, circle time, seminars and recognition of students of outstanding moral values. The course may contain foundational and optional papers in which spiritual and cultural heritage of India and the modern challenges and Health education, yoga asanas, transcendental meditation and moral values in the society in re-structured pattern may be included. It may also be proposed how the integration of topics can be done in languages by inclusion of great personalities of India, their message, their literature in policies by including the topics of ethics by Mahatma Gandhi, Abraham Lincoln, citizens rights and duties and principles of democracy code of conduct etc. In economics, home science and other subjects specific topics need to be included like professional ethics, swadhesi concept and social evils, highlighting the great men and women who have stood for values in political administration and the noble services, including Mother Teresa, excepts from Gita, Bible, Kuran and the verse of Tagore and Gandhi, Sri Aurobindo, Swami Vivekanand, Nehru and Rajaji and ancient scientific researchers in India in different fields as well as the history of great scientists.

Awareness in value assimilation through distance education although seem to be a challenging proposition but experiences of other countries do, however, give indications of its possibilities. A large amount of research studies have flashed strong messages that distance education mode combined with the contact programmes on specific themes (seminars, camps, NSS, scouts and guides etc.) may develop a healthier way of value inculcation.

➤ *Encouraging Development Empirical Research*

It is being widely accepted that meanigful and relevant research has not found its place in the domain of curricular activities taking place at the higher levels of education. The core functions of training, research and teaching are complimentary to each other and thus research, which is a missing link, needs to be made instrumental in the 'reform and revival of education'. Until certain vital components of value education are not researched upon to provide consequential guidelines and proposition, no development can take place. In this resurrection, research has to play a pivotal role in providing the basis for development programmes, policy formulations and training of middle and higher-level human resources. It is with the strong support of empirical evidences on different social, psychological and economical issues that one can rely upon a well thought out plan for implementation of a programme that can go further.

ROLE OF HEAD TEACHER IN THE DEVELOPMENT OF EDUCATIONAL VALUES

Educational Values: We have already seen that Values means primarily to prize, to esteem, to appraise and to estimate. It means the act of achieving something, holding it and also the act of passing judgement upon the nature and amounts of values as compared with something else.

Values are guiding principles of life which are conducive to all round development. They give direction and firmness to life and bring joy, satisfaction and peace to life. Values are like the rails that keep a train on the track and help it move smoothly, quickly and with direction. They bring quality to life. Values cover attitude beliefs, philosophy etc.

There are different types of values. They are cultural values, social values, religious values, moral values, ethial values, political values, education values, etc. Educational values cover many of these values. As education is an (See Chapter 3rd in this book) Educational values cover many of these values. As education is an effective means of social change it includes all these values. As a part and parcel of social system education has to take care of social as well as cultural values. At the same time it has to consider moral, ethical, religious and political values too.

Now value-education is an important part of the educational system. Hence, it is a responsibility of the school or educational institution to impart value education.

HEAD TEACHER is responsible for imparting these educational values. By head teacher we mean the teacher who is in change of the institution.

A efficient, qualified and experienced person has to be appointed a head teacher. His role in this respect is as follows:

1. Academic and administrative management — He must carry out academic functions as well as administrative functions. He must see that through academic activities educational values are properly imparted.
2. Policy planning and providing decision with respect to educational values. For that he must plan for curricular as well as co-curricular activities.
3. Maintaining and evaluation of academic and research activities — He must motivate other teachers to do research on educational values. He must also evaluate their academic and research work. So that he can maintain certain standard in his institution. He must be a guide to everybody. He must provide his consultancy service to all.
4. Promotion of society and institution interaction — He must always try to arrange interaction between society and the institution. So

that both will cooperate to inculcate the educational values for the betterment of the society.

5. Participation Policy Planning at Regional/National level for the development of educational values. He must actively participate in the planning policy at regional and national level.
6. He must provide opportunities to the teacher and students for the development of educational values. He must think of their aptitude, competencies and interest.

For all this he must Vision — he must be able to foresee the growth of the school, society and the nation and then he must start his mission. He must have environment sensitivity and must be able to link the activities of his institution with the society. He must be capable of decision making. He must not deviate from his decision due to any pressure. He must be firm on his own decision. He must have life long learning attitude which will make him aware of the changes taking place in the society and the world at large. The development in the outer world leads to the changes in the educational values. He has to be innovative and creative. Because of this nature he can make his institution innovative and creative. He must listen to his colleague, students and must be sensitive to their problems. Main thing is he must have the qualities of good leadership. So that he can lead his institution on the path of progress.

CONCLUDING REMARKS

The richness in the culture, value, and philosophical ideologies of the trendy country like India is engraved on the sound foundation of value-based education inherited from enriched ancestral possessions. Education at all levels (school, college and university) through all means (direct, indirect or formal and informal) has always been regarded here as a prime means for developing an individual as an integrated whole. At the pre school level, inculcation of values take place but the necessary of value education at the higher education stage percolates from the need to accommodate individual within the desirable accepted societal norms. Taking the model from the ancient scripture of India, the Upanishadh and Gita, wherein emphasis has been laid on the understanding of human beings as an entity of quality, it will definitely be worthwhile to develop an individual with best of abilities. This process can only be initiated at the school level followed by proper grooming at the higher education stage since by that time all competencies are developed and one only needs to be spruced up. Drawing out the best and the capability of applying what is learnt can be more sharpened at this stage. Developing ambience and creating environment becomes imperative at this stage. This nourishment is envisaged to have a multiplier effect in the onward journey as one moves from student life to future challenges.

Recognising the importance of values indoctrination in the institutes of higher learning as also suggested by eminent scholars and thinkers,

NIEPA at the instance of MHRD abd UGC organised a Seminar-cum-Workshop on Education in Human Values and Life Skills in Higher Education. The prime purpose of this workshop was to develop a design of the course to be introduced at university level. The main participants of the seminar were Vice Chancellors drawn from different universities and other institutes of higher learning. In this forum an urgent need for inclusion of a programme on Education in Human Values and Life Skills for students of Higher Education was felt. The major suggested titles were: (*a*) Education of Human Values and Life Skills, (*b*) Art of Living and (*c*) Life Enrichment and Self-Development. The proposed course contents will comprise of seven modules. The essence of each is as follows: (1) Understanding and managing self to make students understand their potentialities and interests and managing self-methods of behaviour modification; (2) Family Life to inculcate human values and rights of all the members; (3) Learning to live together on learning to Live Effectively Amidst Diversity (LEAD); (4) Citizens and Indian Constitution on basic values for citizenship, socialism secular citizenry, justice as a value-social, liberty, equality and dignity of citizens and Judges and others; (5) Transaction to work as preparation of our youth for future avenues in fast changing employment scenario too Leadership on traits, qualities and attributes which help in managing the dynamics of organisations; (7) Indian Art and Culture to cover Indian schools of painting, music, dance and Indian literature.

Orientation to teachers to take up new roles and responsibilities and Counselling to students will form a continuous process in the most organised and professional manner help them to cope with expectations and pressures of emerging demands. One can admit that value orientation at institutes of higher learning is not an impossible proposition. It has to begin with generation of climate conductive to learning and teaching to make value education form a fundamental constituent of a person's life which involves a carefully designed plan of action and activities.

The human brain has the privileged facilities of thinking, imagination and creativity. Computer can store a vast amount of information but it cannot think. Hence, any system of education, unless it is learner-centred, is flexible, is around developing thinking skills and is able to help learners in acquiring the ability of learning, how to learn will gradually lose its relevance. Hence, as Aurobindo has rightly said, 'the first principle of true teaching is that nothing can be taught. The teacher is not an instructor or task master, he is a helper and a guide. His business is to suggest and not to impose.' The teacher does not actually train the pupil's mind but only shows how to perfect the instruments of knowledge. Teacher shows the pupil how to acquire knowledge for himself or herself.

In the Delors' Commission Report, Learning The Treasure Within (1996), Aurobindo's thoughts seem to have been reiterated.

Teachers must adapt their relationship with learners, shifting the emphasis from dispersing information to helping learners seek, organise and manage knowledge.

Today, we see markets flooded with textbooks on subject of 'moral science'. Publishers are rushing to influence the heads of schools. Yet the question is asked at this stage —

- Have these textbooks improved the character of our pupils?
- What is the impact of stories taught during story telling periods?
- Why has selfishness, greed, insensitivity, violence and addiction to drugs increased in our educational institutions?
- Why do pupils carry knives and guns to school?
- Why are pupils of highly disciplined schools caught copying during the examination time?

And there may be many more such querries. What is needed is to review the Value-Education imparted in our schools; and here it is heartening to read in NCERT document —

"EVERY TEACHER HAS TO BE A TEACHER OF VALUES"

9

VALUE-ORIENTED TEACHER EDUCATION

INTRODUCTION

Dr. Radhakrishnan has emphasized that "a civilisation is not built with bricks and motor or any machinery. It is built by men with their quality and character". But, realising a gradual erosion of this, Pandit Jawaharlal Nehru suggested ways and means for the need of the moral and religious education by constituting HIGHER POWER COMMITTEE. Kothari Commission recognised the importance of necessary moral and spiritual values, stated "Modernisation, if it is a living force, must derive its strength from the strength of spirit. Knowledge with lack of essential values in the younger generation is creating many serious, social and ethical conflicts. It is necessary, therefore, and also urgent to make our education value-oriented." The Kothari Commission too has recommended for the introduction of education in moral, social and spiritual values in all educational institutions. In fact, it is the Teacher's Training Colleges that have to take initiative in this regard. Education must blossom human excellence and build human character. Learning how to work together, play together and share decision-making, create and produce together and work through conflicts are the requisite competencies which the citizen of today must possess. It is the Teacher's Training Colleges that help their teacher-educators to terach their pupil-teachers (trainees) learn how to make their judicious use collectively rather than with selfish motives. Behaviour psychologists along with teacher-educators have to collaborate more closely to find out suitable methods of bringing about modification in the attitudes of the students in the schools.

HOW CAN TEACHER EDUCATION BE VALUE ORIENTED?

The current teacher-education programme is neither totally futile nor fully irrelevant. Its objectives as such are limited and orientation is narrow.

Some of the teacher-educators (not all of course!) sometimes (not always of course!) fail to impress upon the trainees regarding the usefulness of the special methods chosen by the trainees and rarely make use of any special method (for instance Geography speical method-master may take his or her trainees to certain places of visit) but just "talk and chalk" method. So too, only a set pattern of lesson-planning with no flexibility in it is followed in practice-teaching programmes. Now, if education means to be a social change, then, the reorientation of our teacher-education programme is a must. For too long, in our teacher-training programmes much stress is put on the cognitive goals of instruction. Hence, the orientation of the teacher's training programme should be put to such a change that it will suit the realistic needs of today. This aspect has been visualised even by National Council For Teacher Education (N.C.T.E.) and stress is put on value-based curriculum. The Value-Oriented Teacher-education will thus have such features that it will have different objectives, and accordingly, a sincere attempt is made here to outline the objectives, to outline the course material to outline the methods and materials and then to outline the entire evaluation programme for value-oriented teacher-education for consideration.

OBJECTIVES OF VALUE-ORIENTED TEACHER EDUCATION WILL MEAN

1. Developing a sort of awareness in trainees about self and society.
2. Inculcating values of self-discipline, self-reliance, truth and honesty etc.
3. Providing opportunities for positive social attitude.
4. Making teacher-trainees sensitive to value-needs of children.
5. Providing awareness about education for peace.

COURSE OF STUDY FOR VALUE ORIENTED TEACHER-EDUCATION

The course of study in teacher-education should

1. Begin with the introduction of values.
2. Have topics related to values in the content of each paper.
3. Should have put emphasis on practical application of each paper.
4. Should have the place for various types of learning experiences inside the class as well as outside the lecture room.

Such a type of course, it is believed, will really be helpful to the trainees in their chosen profession. Method of Instruction for value-oriented Teacher-Education will be such that before the exact teacher-training starts in the college, there should be an orientation programme for the trainees during the beginning of week. This will help them to higher goals of teacher-education than mere job preparation. Further, teacher-educators should use progressive methods of teaching that will involve trainees in discussion, activities, projects, practicals and also for an independent study; field trips and co-curricular activities. Further, invitation should be given to experts in moral values, yoga etc. to deliver lectures which will enlighten the pupil teachers in learning more about the values of truth, goodness, etc.

Materials and Media For Value-Oriented Teacher Education should be such where teaching aids, slides and films may be prepared and also used by the trainees. The trainees must also be made aware regarding the Radio and T.V. programmes connected with values and value-education. So too, exhibition and display of value-oriented writings, pictures and posters should be held regularly in the Teachers' Training Colleges. Further, biographies of great people and great scholars should not only be read but also discussed in the lecture halls, once in a fortnight to propagate the values that they carried through their lives.

Scheme of Evaluation To Be Done For Value-Oriented Teacher Education Programme should be a broad-based evaluation for testing value-education. Besides the written tasks, group discussions conducted by a panel of judges should be given due weightage. So too, the faculty-improvement programmes is essential for teacher-educators. In this regard, it may be stated that the conferences pertaining to value-education arranged either at the National or even at the International level must be attended by the teacher-educators for their professional enrichment.

VALUE-ORIENTED TEACHER EDUCATION

Teacher Education has now assumed a great social importance and has therefore been the target of severe criticism. It is being reviewed and recognised in every state with the help of an enriched curriculum, better techniques of teaching and evaluation and even addition of several new courses of social significance like population education, national integration, community services, rural development, moral and religious education, etc. With all these efforts, the present teacher education still remains to be isolated and incomplete. It is isolated from the society and its aspirations. Kothari Commission points out that the teacher education suffers from three types of isolation:

- Isolation from University life,
- Isolation from Schools,
- Isolation from one another.

But worse than that is the fact that it suffers from the isolation from society. This isolation makes teacher education incomplete, valueless and worthless in our developing country.

In order to make education responsive to the new needs of the society, Teacher Education has to be reoriented in its aim and approach, curriculum and content. In this regard, the working group of University Education for Seventh Five Year Plan (1985-90) has emphatically suggested that Value-orientation in education should constitute a special thrust in the Seventh Plan for Teacher Education in particular. The opinion of experts too was in favour of value-orientation for teachers because —

a. A teacher has a unique position,

b. A teacher has a key to knowledge,

c. A teacher has a multiplier effect,

d. A teacher has a social prestige and

e. A teacher provides a model to younger generation.

Hence, it is very essential that the teachers under training in the Teachers Training Colleges, should be well exposed to value-education during their training.

The functional value-oriented education should have the following features:

a. It must be integrated with syllabus and text books.

b. It must be handled by teacher-educators with fact and imagination.

c. It must be reflected in the behaviour of teacher-educators and pupil-teachers in their day-to-day functioning.

d. It must be taught to pupil-teachers through various co-curricular activities organised very meaningfully by the Teacher-educators.

e. It must be fully operative and functional at all stages with pre-service and in-service orientation.

TASK OF TEACHER EDUCATORS

Now comes the actual task of teacher-educators particularly from Teachers' Training Colleges. It is very essential for these teacher-educators to give a proper training to those pupil teachers who are involved in Value-education. Such would-be-teachers, (i.e. teacher-trainees) should be given a clear idea of the meaning as well as significance of the terms like 'value-judgement', 'value-dilemma', 'value-conflict' and 'value-criterion'. An assertion that the individual makes on the basis of his or her values, are termed as value-judgements. For instance, the teacher-educators should specifically make their trainees understand that whenever any assignment given to the pupils by the respective teachers is expected to be given on time, it means then, these teachers are making value-judgements. The value-criterion that supports this judgement may be school-discipline or even a respect of punctuality. Such things may be brought out by the Teachers Training Colleges through their Inernship Programmes. Each trainee may be asked to handle ten-ten students from one and the same division continuously for one full week. In the same manner the teacher-trainees had to be given a clear understanding regarding Value-Conflicts or Value-Dilemma, etc. While teaching the topics of 'Emotions and Sentiments', the teacher-educator may make the teacher-trainees understand clearly about the concept of 'Master-Sentiment'. When a person is in conflict while faced with two values and a question is "which to choose?" then, there is within him or her a 'Value-Conflict'. The individual will select or choose that which permits his or her conscience.

A glance at our educational system will tell us how far our educational institutions have been successful in making value-education an integral part of education in the vast majority of our schools. Though attempts are being made towards it, the methods of value-education are largely such that encourage memorisation and rote-learning rather than responsible personal decision-making. Main strategies for imparting value-education could be child-centered, teacher-centered and experimental learning strategies. Our Value-Education Programmes (VEP) should aim at autonomy — a stage of purely internal, moral development, a period of self-rule for the individual who imposes moral codes on himself or herself by himself or herself.

Today's youth are faced with several hang-ups and are suffering from prejudices of class and caste divisions, the corrupting influences of money and power, etc. resulting in social chaos and entering into the sanctity of family relationship. Now, here comes the significance of Value-Orientation-Education. It is the Value-Orientation-Education that will make our children aware of the implication of stresses and tensions and create in them resilience of mind to fight these and lead a life of mental equipoise.

Education that does not awaken our children against moral and social turpitude, does not serve the real purpose howsoever much it may succeed in fighting their minds with facts and formulae. This is what our teacher-educators have to keep in mind while giving training to their pupil-teachers.

APPROACHES TO VALUE-ORIENTED EDUCATION

Many a time, a question is raised by people asking — "How should one develop a set of values free from the influence of any external forces?" Is it possible to train children to base their values on reasoning?" Answers to such questions lies in approaches to value-clarification. Value-clarification is an approach to value-oriented education which facilitates the selection and internalisation of values. In the words of Sidney B. Simon (1974), the essential purpose of value-clarification is to freely choose values, to vivaciously cherish them, to vitally affirm them and positively enact them.

According to Howe and Howe (1975) the value-clarification approach helps students learn:

1. To choose their values freely,
2. To choose their values from alternatives,

3. To choose their values after weighing the consequence of each alternative,
4. To prize and cherish their values,
5. To share and publicly affirm their values,
6. To act upon their values and
7. To act upon their values repeatedly and consistently.

In the process of learning different curricular subjects, one comes to imbibe certain values, habits of thought, qualities of mind that are concomittant to the pursuit of that particular knowledge field.

In other words, value-education spans the entire learning, cultivation of imagination, strengthening of will and training of character. When we so relate value-education to education, we can identify the approach as one of the integrating values into the very fabric of education. The key of survival of the species 'Human Being', values such as love, cooperation, trust, acceptance, dignity, joy, compromise, understanding truth, etc. must be taught. This means, teaching human values is teaching survival skills.

Hence, value-education should not be taught in isolation. It is the very purpose of life. It is an approach to life. It is a prescription for happy living. It is a programme that committed itself to human undestanding. Value-education helps in the development of human personality which, in turn, have five domains or levels i.e., physical, intellectual, emotional, psychological and spiritual. Corrresponding to these are the five values —

Physical	-	Rightens conduct
Intellectual	-	Truth
Emotional	-	Peace
Psychological	-	Love
Spiritual	-	Non-violence

The integral development of all five domains is what any scheme of education must aim at. At primary stage, the instructions should be imparted through stories, including stories from great religions of the world. At the secondary stage, there may be frequent discussions between teachers and the student. The school atmosphere, personality and behaviour of the teachers, the facilities provided in the school, will have great importance in developing a sense of values.

ROLE OF THE TEACHER

Since time immemorial, importance of values in the life of a person have been discussed. As a matter of fact, the Value-Education Programme strongly believes that value-education truly begins with the teacher. Hence, it is true to say that a teacher cannot really be a teacher unless he or she is committed to the progression. Now, among teachers too, the area and responsibility varies. It is the teacher of the primary classes who holds the key. Primary teacher is the one around whom the programme of education in value-education revolves, and it is the Primary teacher who lays the foundation for building the students' personality. This does not mean, however, that the rersponsibility of other level of teachers in any less.

If the very concept of the word value is to be made known to the student world in the true sense of the term, then, the school must start working on the proper line. It is with this view the Government of Maharashtra have now introduced the scheme of implementation of value-education from Std. I to Std. X.

The emphasis on education for inculcation of values imposes on the teacher a very special responsibility. Values can best be imparted by the living examples of the teachers by evolving themselves a high standard of self-discipline. Again, since there is explosion of knowledge, teachers will have to be trained in the art of life-long education, and in the art of learning to learn. So too, special programmes for training to pupil teachers from Teaachers' Training Colleges should be formulated which will provide greater awareness of responsibilities in regard to inculcation values in schools. Considering that the teacher is the real bridge between the past and the future and the carrier of cultural heritage from generation to generation, it must be expected from every teacher to become a prepetual student of the lessons of history and of the quest of knowledge by which greater future can be built through inculcation of value-education in schools.

Today, we are speaking of child-centered education, but only the teacher can really give concrete shape to this concept. For, it is only the teacher who can introduce the dynamic methods that would place the child in the centre of the learning process.

In view of what has been said above, the role of the teacher will be —

a. To observe his or her students, their inclinations and capacities, so as to be able to help them with deep sympathy and understanding.

b. To become an animator rather than a mere lecturer.

c. To inspire much rather than to instruct.

d. To help the students by process of suggestion and develop in them inner will to grow and progress.

Values in education is a multidimensional concept. Value is related to every aspect of education. Value has a power that can unite learners, teachers and also community. The very purpose of education is to help human beings draw out their built in generative power. Rabindranath Tagore has rightly stated — "The highest mission of education is to help us to realise the inner principles of unity of all knowledge and all the activities of our social and spiritual being", whereas, Sri Aurobindo says

— "the first principle of teaching is that nothing can be taught. The teacher is not an instructor or task-master, but is a helper and a guide."

In fact, the teacher has more than one role to play —

1. The teacher has to play the role of a facilitator and cooperative enterprise in which the different types of courses occur through reciprocal give and take.
2. The teacher must have a concern for disadvantaged pupils.
3. The teacher is expected to arouse enthusiasm.
4. The teacher should act as a source of inspiration, and should be enthusiastic about his or her own work.
5. The teacher must be a communicator of love and knowledge.
6. The teacher must be able to differentiate between power and duty.
7. The teacher must be always an honest endeavour.
8. The teacher should make a sincere attempt to understand his or her pupils, their needs, their interests, their abilities, their aptitudes and their problems.
9. The teacher should set his or her own values as far as students are concerned.
10. The teacher should have sensitivity for gender equality.

Fraenkel (1977) discussed some kind of procedure and techniques which he based on the belief that "being able to identify, able to analyse and able to assess" are the important abilities that one should possess. Hence, a continuing analysis and assessment of all alternatives (during hard circumstances) in schools could help develop the abilities to identify, analyse and assess.

Felix Coikara in his book "Live Your Values", a resource book for value-education speaks of 10 commandments. They are worth quoting here as a source of inspiration to our value-education teachers. These are —

1. The teacher should prepare for his lessons very carefully.
2. The teacher should try to understand the needs, desires, problems and struggles of his or her students.
3. The teacher should listen to the students with love, empathy and understanding, i.e. he or she should be tolerant.
4. The teacher should be honest in sharing his or her experiences with the students.
5. The teacher should accept the ideas of the students with appreciation.
6. The teacher should be firm in maintaining discipline even in fun.
7. The teacher should try to understand the language of the students.

8. The teacher should be flexible to change the sessions as per the needs of the students.
9. The teacher should create an atmosphere of warmth and freedom.
10. The teacher should believe in the good will of his or her students.
11. The teacher should encourage the spirit of inquiry.
12. The teacher should pay attention to pupils' personal hygiene.

It was Coleridge who observed that "man may be made better not a consequence of education but during the very process of education". The value-orientation must become an integral part of the entire education system by weaving the value into the entire curricular programmes. It has to be done from the early stage of education in order to have a lasting effect on the future conduct and the way of life of the adult. Appropriate educational approaches and systematic teaching strategies spontaneously cultivate the inculcation of values. Learning will get any meaning or even any purpose only when values inhere them. Hence, certain cardinal approaches have to be borne in mind. Childhood as well as the studenthood is purely a period of intellectual curiosity about facts. At this stage, free and frank discussion about values will feed their curiosity and awaken in them the sense of imbibing them. Each student must be made self-reliant to uphold his or her personal and social values. In this connection, temptation is there to quote the words of Bhagwan Satya Sai Baba —

"Value for education, education for life:

Life for love, love for man:

Man for service, service for spirituality:

Spirituality for society, society for nation:

Nation for world, world for peace!"

Really, how very true!

"The end and aim of all educational training", says Swami Vivekananda "is to make the man good for the full development of man". This needs to have that pattern of education which combines —

Gandhiji's Karmayoga

Tagore's Anandyoga

Aurobindo's Poornayoga

CONCLUDING REMARKS

Concludingly, it may be said then that, if the teacher is to play his or her right role in the production of value-oriented education, the teacher himself or herself has to be value-oriented. It is only when he is himself or herself value-oriented, that he or she will be able to give the necessary inspiration, help, guidance to his or her students. As we all know, values cannot be taught merely by discourses, just as swimming cannot be taught merely by lectures. A good teacher of swimming has to be a swimmer himself or herself and should be able to take the learner into the waters to make the learner swim. Similarly, a teacher of values should himself or herself be a seeker and aspirant of values and should be ready to walk with the learner on the long and difficult path of realising and embodying values.

However, a request to say that today it is really difficult to find teachers, who, by their exemplary behaviour can influence their pupils. Yet, we have to agree with the fact that the teacher has an important place in the cultivation of values among pupils.

PROFESSIONAL VALUES AND TEACHER-EDUCATION

10

When a question is asked — 'who is a human being?'; and as an answer to this question, it is said — 'A human being is the supreme creation of God.' But soon next question jumps up like a boomerang — 'Is human being maintaining his or her supremacy?' In the present scenerio, is he or she behaving as per the rules and regulations in the society? Such questions really remain without any satisfactory answer! In today's materialistic and scientific age, men and animals do not seem to be different from each other. However, only one characteristic differentiates them. It is intelligence. A human being can think. He or she knows what is good and what is bad. He or she also knows what is right and what is wrong. Such differentiation animals cannot make. But a human being can. Yet, regret to note that today's people have become more materialistic, more money-minded and more and more concerned with his or her own beliefs and benefits. There is absolutely no time for him or her to think of others. People have become so self-centred that they cannot see the sorrows of others. Hence, it is correctly said that today people have completely lost the cultural values! Education is usually looked upon as an organised, purposive activity with pre-established goals. But in reality it does not seem to be so. In fact, education is essentially the art of learning, not only from books but from the whole movement of life. Good education is that which helps pupils to deal with life as a whole, and as helps them to discover lasting values. True and good education helps the pupils to discover true values which come as unbiased investigation and self-awareness.

Gloabally, there is an overwhelming concern over the quality and relevance of education. The progress of a country depends on the quality of education which further depends on the quality of teachers and teacher-education system. Teaching is considered as one of the noblest profession and the teacher is of paramount importance in the field of education. The teacher is the key person on whom depends the future of mankind. In fact, teachers can do miracles, which can shape raw material into a finished product. As Chanaya has rightly said —

However, for this, a teacher has to be conscious of his or her role model, through his or her conduct, action and adherence to human values.

In fact, every profession has certain values attached to it; and a person can do justice to his or her profession, if he or she obeys those values. Hence, professional laws are very essential for becoming a good teacher. A good teacher is non-stop learner to play his or her role effectively. On account of this, role of the present-day teacher has become very challenging, complex and multifaceted. The challenges can be easily met if the teacher works towards his or her profession with commitment and obeys the professional laws. In fact, a teacher's job is more difficult than the recognised professionalists. Professional ethics demands that a teacher should not try to exploit school influence for private gains. The all-round development of the pupils depends upon the professional competency and efficiency of teachers. Professional values for teachers measure all the characteristics of teaching profession like responsibilities, attitudes, honesty, fairness, integrity, diligence, loyalty, cooperation, justice, faithfulness, respect for others and self, teaching procedures, assessment of students and conduct of behaviour. In today's atmosphere of competency, proper training of teachers is very essential. Because this helps them to inculcate desirable values in their pupils. Teacher is not merely a given of information; but he or she is the one who points the way to wisdom and truth. Good teachers maintain the perfect equality betweeen them and the pupils; and it is they who create read freedom in the institution. Education and significance of life must be synthesized, because peace starts in the individual and then grows into world peace!

Because of the above said facts teacher must be provided value-oriented education; and teachers' training institutes should develop ethical values through seminar, training and colloquium. There should be inservice training for teacher-educators.

Because a teacher has to discharge unlimited responsibilities, he or she must be very much well-versed with all types of professional values. Hence, a teacher must necessarily have good knowledge of values. In fact, values should become the core of teacher education without which education is not at all considered complete.

STATUS OF HIGHER EDUCATION AND HUMAN VALUES

11

It is unfortunate that even after so many years of India's independent rule, the pattern of higher education continues to be as the British bequeathed to us. A close scrutiny of the curriculum of various academic programmes will show that except for a little tinkering here and there, it has remained unchanged. Three commissions and many committees set up to devise new strategies in an attempt to modernise education, have come up with rosy blueprints for various schemes for quality education. Not much has changed. British legacy lingers on, although there are bright patches of qualitative work across the country where some universities and other centres of higher learning have distinctive achievements to their credit. But this is like a oasis in a vast desert of indifference and status quoism. Hence, it is a matter of serious concern and calls for introspection at all levels to ensure effective and efficacious remedies to usher in value based education — education that matters, educational that promotes human excellence and education that is globaly competitive.

India is the largest democracy and the 2nd largest system of higher education in the world. There are 256 universities and more than 10,000 colleges. Every eighth student enrolled for higher education in the world is an Indian. But it is disheartening to note that only 6% of the relevant age group, i.e., 18-23 years, find their way to centres of higher learning. It is further estimated that these lucky ones mostly come from 30% of the elite and upper middle class groups, thus depriving a major chunk of the poor of the fruits of higher education.

But the moot question is whether those enrolled for higher education are getting the right type of training, well equipped laboratories, proper facilities for research and so on. If so, why does India continue to stagnate? Obviously, all is not well with the state of education. Hence, it is the bounden duty of the teachers, the parents, the Governments and the planners of education and various voluntary agencies to see that these young boys and girls prosper intellectually and simultaneously become good human beings free from the traints of arrogance, hatred and intolerance.

It is true that students must get a chance to learn more than one skill in the course of formal education. Even cafeteria mode should be introduced to create all kinds of avenues for the learners. Information and Communication technologies today have revolutionised the world. Computerisation and digital storage and transformation of information and instruction have far-reaching implications for the educational process. This obviously means that access to information has vastly increased. In the open universities, the sending of course material through the post has been replaced with E-mailing of the same through Internet.

Moreover, globalisation is the key word. Competitiveness is the order of the day. In an era of 'Affluent Consumerism', lust for power is gaining ascendancy. Corruption like malignant cancer is vitiating and destroying the entire social fabric. Our society seems to have been caught up in this malaise. This is where the role of the universities comes in. Not that the university dons hold a magic wand to stem the rising tide of this 'grab and run' system, yet a sincere effort to inculcate value system is urgently called for.

Intellectualism sans humanism is of little substance. Students come to the colleges and the universities with a desire to learn and gather intellectual wealth. They come out of the universities and reinvest this intellectual wealth in the society. Their knowledge, research, skills and intellectualism constitute public capital for the benefit of the society. The universities are hallowed places where teachers and students are the custodiams of the rich intellectual and technological wealth for its onward transmission for the welfare of the nation at large.

However, all this will be possible if our system of education is based on finer values of life. Benefit of these values, and without any sympathy to the miseries of the oppressed for other vulnerable sections, our intellectuals will be out of tune in terms of needs and aspirations of the society. It may be noted that all that the mankind has achieved and in spite of all our glittering trophies of materialstic prosperity, it can be ruefully admitted that we in T. S. Elliot's words, "are in the world confused and dark disturbed by portents of fear". We can get out of this rut by clinging to our faith in human values. Our education must be punctuated and governed by a system of values, which would indisputably lead to full flowering of the individuals in the society. The document of new policy of education asserted that, "The growing concern over erosion of essential values and increasing cynicism in society has brought into focus the need for a readjustment in the curriculum in order to make education a forceful tool for the cultivation of moral and social values".

But what are these values? Philosophers and Educationists over the ages have identified 'Happiness', 'Goodness', 'Truth' and 'Beauty' as ultimate values, the values which do not change fundamentally from generation to generation, society to society and culture to culture. Then there are moral values like honesty, tolerance, justice, self-control, compassion, freedom and so on. These enable the man to control his lower primitive and animal instincts so that he can emulate certain ideals, which are available in plenty in our rich cultural heritage. Therefore, an educational system should be evolved in which these values are incorporated and through constant interaction and dialogue, the teacher is able to imprint on the young formative minds under their guidance, the paramount importance of these values.

However, the values of 'tolerance' and 'compassion' are the panacea of all ills confronting our social order today. Intolerance is the backbone of our social and political system. Jayaprakash Narayan, once said "Dissent is the essence of democracy". If we can learn to be tolerant to each other's point of view, religious bigotry, caste conflicts and racial prrejudices will disappear. Various incidents of violence in Bihar, Orissa, U.P., Maharashtra and Gujarat have only brought into focus our sense of intolerance and disrespect to each other's point of view. Secondly, 'compassion' for the poor and disadvantaged sections of society must flow from the affluent sections of the society in a natural manner. Saints, Seers, and Sages have spoken of divine compassion in "human compassion". Gandhiji warned that 'riches' of the rich are under their care and custody for its proper sharing and distribution amongst the poor and have-nots.

A dialogue of absorbing interest between Gandhiji and Tagore epitomizes Gandhiji's concern for poor in India. Tagore said, "Gandhiji, are you so unromantic? When in the early dawn, the morning sun rises, does it not fill your heart with joy to see its reddish glow? When the birds sing does not your heart thrill with its divine music? When the rose opens its petals and bloom in the garden does its sight not bring cheer to your heart." The Mahatma replied, "Gurudev, I am not so dumb or insensitive, as not to be moved by the beauty of rose or the morning rays of the sun or the divne music of the birds. But what can I do? My one desire, my one anxiety, my one ambition is when shall I see the red tint of the rose on the cheeks of hungry naked millions of my people? When shall I hear the sweet and melodious song of the birds in place of their agonizing sighs? When will such music come out of their soul and when will that day come when the light of the morning sun will illumine the heart of the common man in India? When will I see its luster and brightness on his face"?

The condition is no different today than when Gandhiji wrote the above lines. But where is the remedy? Universities provide an open platform for democratization. In fact, it is an experiment in living together. The students come from different classes, castes and family backgrounds, sit in the same classroom learn the same lesson and eat the same food in the hostels. They together generate intellectual wealth to enrich social and economic fabric of the nation. They attain perfection as scientists, researchers, technologies and entrepreneurs. It is the teacher who gives them this and much more. It is the teacher again who has to tell them to tolerant and compassionate. It is the teacher again who has to tell them to be tolerant and compassionate. It is the teacher who has to inculcate in his students a sense of responsible citizenship. It is he who has to invest them with the rich cultural heritage of India and its finer values of life. It is the teacher again who has to set certain ideals before his students. Votaries of pragmatic materialism scoff at ideals. But Albert Einstine emphasised "The power of 'Ideals' is incalculable. We see no power in a drop of water. But once it turns into ice inside the rock, it splits the rock. Turning into steam, it drives the piston of the most powerful engine". Such is the power of the ideals. The teacher has to give these ideals.

All of us must recognise that one of the important corollary of education is culture. Education by itself cannot produce culture and not all eduated people can call themselves cultured. Tagore while comparing education and culture compared eduation with the precious stone of diamonds while culture with the light it reflects. While the stone has weight, the light has glow. There is no greater wealth then wisdom; no greater poverty than ignorance; no greater heritage than culture. Culture teaches us to be selfless, kind and compassionate. We have a difficult situation; a situation where wealth is worshipped as God and pride has become a creed. Selfishness is entrenched in the intellect; the ego is flaunted and desires have become an adorment. Compassion has dried up. Hypocrisy has become the hallmark of life. But if our emphasis is on improving 'Quality of Life' rather than on 'Quality of living', the task of transformation and reconstruction of the social order will become easier, and educational endeavour will flourish in an equitable social order.

12

PLAN OF ACTION (STRATEGIES) TO BE ADOPTED FOR INCULCATION OF VALUES IN SCHOOLS

INTRODUCTION

Historically, interest in values among philosophers and educators dates back to 3rd Century B.C. when Aristotle, the leading Greek Educational Philosopher showed great interest in character-building and development of values related to knowledge-growth of the pupils. In fact, there was never any time in the history of education that the educational thinkers ever separated education from values. Value-education was always considered as an integral part of education programme. In fact, inculcation of desirable values is not a matter of imparting knowledge (regarding values) alone, but suitable skills and attitudes are to be developed through both curricular and curricular programmes. The pupils ought to appreciate the values and reflect them in their conduct and behaviour in and outside the school. Values are something that are desirable and worth of esteem for their own sake. Human values are those values which help human beings to live in harmony with the world. Education, so to say, is a vast circle, and what we propose for one sector of education for inculcation of values, is applicable to other sectors of education also. If we wish our teachers to be value-oriented, then we should tone up our teachers' training programmes. We want our teacher-educators to train our pupil-teachers so that they will be rightly equipped as vehicles of values for children in schools. By this, it is meant that a teacher is a messenger, transmitter and a carrier. Our determination of what the teacher has to transmit is dependent upon what we determine to be valuable for our children. This point has to be kept in view in the outline of a possible programme for value-oriented education. The need for value-education has been emphasised time and again — However, the question now is — How do we go about helping our pupils in value-development through the process of value-education?

On the basis of the above discussion, a sincere attempt has been made in this chapter to provide the teachers with different types of vehicles through which they convey effectively to the students' different values. Values exist in people's minds and these are such invaluable ideas of life which people adore and like to live until they die. Hence, it is the responsibility of the teacher to inculcate the values among their pupils very tactfully. In fact, values could be reckoned on the unparallel ideas of human beings with which one can exhibit extraordinary courage and fortitude when surrounded by turmoil and failure. Therefore, a lucid explanation will surely develop understanding of values to the students and at the same time may lead to develop moral reasoning which is another way of implementing values among pupils. The choices of the students are critical not only for their own happiness and well-being at the present but also for their future. The value-activities to be provided, should, therefore, be the samples of exploration exercise in which the students can be engaged. Every subject in the syllabus is, in fact, an arena to examine values and their effects.

The purpose of the activities is to have students think about values and their practical implications as well as to further their understanding and hence commitment to positive values. This will happen through recognition of the importance of values and of their own responsibility in making positive and personal choices. Through practical application, students will develop social skills as well as cooperative behaviour.

Now, varieties of the value-activities can be used by teachers as well as by pupil-teachers (during their internship programme). All such value-activities, which will be discussed in the current chapter are just a beginning. The teachers are requested to expand their own creativity, expertise, cultural and educational resources. With regards to this, it may be said that a true teacher is one who is always a learner. While teaching of facts makes man wise, the teaching of values make one truly human. Everywhere, and at all times, education has been built on value-system, conducive to the development of physical, intellectual, emotional and spiritual life.

INCORPORATING VALUES THROUGH THE EXISTING CURRICULUM

No wonder, values are very much important and need to be projected. But what is needed is that they have to be filtered and installed through in a way that do not become sermons or moral preaching as such. One must, therefore, note that there are varieties of activities that may be undertaken lying under each value. Teacher as a content-expert, will decide which materials on hand may best portray the values. Teachers know what touches their students.

Some of the activities are discussed, but let us make a beginning with prayer.

PRAYER

Prayer is there in almost all the schools before the regular school period starts. Prayer must be held in mother tongue in proper, calm atmosphere and may be recited by both teacher and students.

At the secondary level, particularly, value-education happens effectively through those teachers, who willingly and creatively choose to incorporate values through the regular curriculum.

GEOGRAPHY (SOCIAL STUDIES)

Geography is such a subject that can easily lend to value-discussion. The teacher may stop at a critical point during teaching and either one student or a group of students may be asked to exercise choice and then, let it be pointed out that individual choice is important. In the teaching of Geography care has to be taken to associate the learner with the nature, observation of the natural phenomenon could inspire them to realise the inherent justice, regulation and order freedom and discipline.

LITERATURE

All the values (listed by Government of Maharashtra for the inculcation in schools) are the characteristics of leading a good life and these can be easily achieved by making the children read good literature. In the language periods, the teacher can select the reading materials which relate to the value being explored. The material that is included her are poems, short stories, autobiographies, philosophical writings or the current books in which the heroine or hero demonstrates the value that is in focus.The students will be asked to react to the materials they just read, to write about the value or to make-up their own poems (particularly in Std. IX and X). Some of the values that have been stressed through good literature are —

- Money may be a measure of success in the material world, but one should be generous in handling it, at this is not an end in itself?
- If everyone tries to do one's best, competition is bound to be there, but one must try to play fair. He or she who tries to play fair, wins through in the end.
- Evil contains the seeds of its punishment and destruction.
- Children should work together to accomplish their goals.
- One must give respect to one's elders and gain their blessings.
- It is hard work that pays and makes the person win.

Literature, by virtue of being imaginative, is capable to promote discussion. Because, when children read, their own imaginations are formed and their imagination enforces their ideals. Literature, in all its products and forms (as history, story etc.) modify these ideals and has a lasting influence. A poem or a novel or a drama definitely stimulates the thoughts of the readers. Developing children's interest in reading is not a simple task. Teachers have to take lot of initiative to create a craze and love for reading in the minds of children.

Concludingly, it may be said then that if reading of book is that influential, then, it may be firmly stated that the educationists, authors, teachers, evaluators, librarians and even parents must be gided in the first instance by what will interest the most and by what best represents the values.

There are still many other activities or many other varieties of methods and modalities that can be used, and students should be asked to —

- Reflect on effects of each positive value.
- Experience values through play, cooperative games and songs.
- Study different subject areas and apply respective values to those areas.
- Experience values artistically through drama, dance, songs — verbally or in written form through debate, discussion, essay, story writing, etc.

There are still few more activities for the inculcation of values is by participation of students in cultural activities like drama, debate, story-telling, story-writing, essays, poetry recitation, celebration of national songs, organisation of sports, music, games. Let us talk about drama now.

DRAMA

Drama is a wonderful medium to incorporate values. Therefore, the teacher has to select those plays that have to do with the pertaining of values. Students have to be encouraged to select their favourite songs and this would need to be done locally because of the diversity of languages — Marathi, Urdu, Kannada, Tamil, Gujarati....etc. and also on the availability of the material. The age level of students is also to be taken into consideration. Through drama-activity, students very easily become acclimatised to "acting out" certain situations, taking various roles and looking as solution.

One must note that in all there are 3 important approaches for inculcation of values —

Teaching of values through suggestion

Teaching of values through participation and

Teaching of values through examples.

The best example of teaching of values through participation is drama-activity. In fact, the spirit of values is ingrained in all the activities of the students under the able guidance of their teachers. In many cases, students discover values with the help of their teachers. Hence, students must be inspired to play a drama. Dramatization has to be used with the purpose of exposing the particular traits in the character and appealing upon their appreciation.

Activities that have been discussed so far, should have cultural, social and national impact on the impressionable and tender minds at their formative stage. Paricipation in the varied activities, quoted so far, will give the students fresh and first-hand experiences which will be helpful in extending not only the mental horizon of the pupils but also broadening their hearts, deepening the sense of duty, social obligation, nationalism, internationalism and humanism.

Participation of students in school assembly, curricular and cocurricular activities, celebrations of national and religious festivals, work experiences, team games and sports, social service camps, can help them in inculcating the values of co-operation, mutual regards, honesty, integrity, discipline and social responsibility.

SCIENCE

The subject of science can be very neatly tackled by the science teachers for the inculcation of values among the students particulalry of Std. V and Std. VI. Certain striking facts like extraordinary phenomena of intelligence in animals and birds has to be brought out by the teacher. As the students enter into higher standards (classes) the quality of sensitivity, silencing the mind and intense search for truth have to be specifically told to the students. Development of the concept of value-consciousness should be made to proceed steadily right from Std. I. Values like maintaining punctuality, cleanliness and orderliness may be made clear to students while teaching the subject of science particularly while teaching a topic like 'Human Body'. Accordingly, good habits like doing exercises and playing on the playground regularly, will be developed in the students.

VALUE-INCULCATION THROUGH COCURRICULAR ACTIVITIES

The prime purpose of education is to develop all dimensions of the human intellect so that our students can help make our country a more democractic cohesive, socially responsible, culturally rich, ecologically sustainable and internationally competitive nation. All such things can be achieved in a true sense of the term if there is a proper inculcation of values in schools. As discussed earlier, it can be done through curricular subjects, but the inculcation of values can also be done through conducting various cocurricular activities. The task for the implementation of values into existing curricular is to assist teachers in making explicit values into their daily classroom programmes. A plan of action is required which links the rhetoric to existing practice. Value must be experienced in social interaction and reinforced by curriculum content and process. Students need an opportunity to explore the relationship between personal meaning and the shared values of society and this can be well done through different approaches inclusive of few narrative approaches using story-telling, story-writing, debate, discussion, role-playing, etc.

Before going into details regarding cocurrilcular activities, it must be noted that the cocurricular activities must focus on value-inculcation rather than on winning prizes. In this regard, let us have a look at the following table:

ACTIVITY	VALUE
1. Visit and observe nearby planetarium.	Quest for knowledge, spirit of enquiry, scientific temper.
2. Take pupils to nearby forests and make them observe different types of tress and animals.	Love towards nature responsibility and protection of environment.
3. Make a visit to the fields producing different food crops.	Food value.
4. Encourage stamp collection.	Curiosity can develop the value of collecting new and old items.
5. Arrange seminars, debates and workshops.	Participation, encouraging the communication skill, etc.
6. Writing diary.	Self-control
7. Special assembly in schools.	Cooperation, time consciousness' good manner, national consciousness, obedience, regularity and sincerity.
8. Stories	Anti-unsociability, equality, faithfulness, gentle manners, justice, kindness, non-violence, and responsibility.
9. Celebrating national festivals of different religions.	Unit of diversity.
10. Prayer and meditation.	Devotion to God, self-discipline, self-realisation and control of senses.
11. Shramadan.	Hard work, gratitude, service, friendship and dutifulness.
12. Annual excursions.	Sharing of ideas, cordiality, love towards nature and creativity.

ACTIVITY	VALUE
13. Competition in sports and games.	Sportsmanship, team spirit and tolerance.
14. Cultural programmes.	Cultural and moral values.
15. Silence.	Control of speech.

DEVELOPMENT OF VALUE-CONSCIOUSNESS THROUGH STORY (followed by lot of discussion)

The teacher may either tell the story or may ask the students to develop the story by giving them certain points.

Through interacting with story, students are given the opportunity to reason about the cause and effect of actions, and to consider moral choices. Examining values through story response allows students to explore issues, which may be problematic or contemptuous, without necessarily taking emotional burdens involve upon themselves. Story provides a distancing effect while still allowing the issues to be confronted. Students may use the world of story as a mirror for their own life experiences. Students may be asked to relate issues to their own life experience and speculate as to how they might handle or have handled in a different manner.

Although a story implies the author's intentions, interpretation is an individual experience. Students need to be encouraged to identify their own experiences with others in order to make more informal personal decisions. Through interaction with story, students can consider characters' actions, perspectives and motives and make judgements about them. They may then relate the story to experiences in their own lives so that they can begin to understand the influences on the decisions they make.

Approach through story (for the inculcation of value) paves the way for thinking skills approach because story response stimulates students to discuss issues at a deep level. Sample questions may include —

- What is the purpose of the story? Theme, moral, perspective, etc.
- What choices did the character/s have?
- What situations helped/hindered the character/s in their choices?
- What circumstances were beyond the control of the character/s?
- List the range of consequences for their various choices available to the characters.
- Make judgements about these actions and consequences.
- Think of a similar situation that you know about or have been in —

  1. What did you do?
  2. Would you do the same thing again?

3. Why?/Why not?
4. Did your decision benefit you?
5. Did your decision affect any one else? How?

- What stops/helps you to make decisions which benefit others/ yourself?
- Do you need any external stimulus (reward or punishment) to help you make decisions?

Particularly for Std. I and II stories may be taken up for the development of the themes like — (i) the ideal of truth, (ii) aspiration for perfection etc. For such themes, the teacher may narrate the stories of Raja Harishchandra or of Mahatma Gandhi or any other that is concerned with the theme. The children of this tender age can be helped to understand the sayings like 'To speak the truth, whatever the consequences' or 'where truth alone prevails, beauty and goodness pervade'.

The, special exhibitions based on such stories may also he arranged on the said themes. In the end, the teacher may recommend certain exercises to the pupils and ask them to practice.

As the students enter into higher classes, the development of value-consciousness can be done through a study of the —

A. Stories of Bodhisatva from the "Jatakas".
B. Parables from Bible.
C. Questions put to Yudhishtira on the bank of the lake and his answers.
D. Message received by Prophet Muhammad from the Angel.
E. Account of Rabindranath Tagore's experience of his opening to poetic inspiration.
F. "Powers of the Mind" from Swami Vivekananda.

In the same manner, the stories based on the values like Dignity of Labour, Equality of Sex, Punctuality, etc. may be taken up by the teacher for the inculcation of values. If a ready story is not available even in the books like. Supplementary Readers, the teacher may create (write) his or her own story and then cyclostyle the same for futher activity.

MAKING USE OF ROLE PLAY

This cocurricular Role-Play Activity can be taken up for all the classes right from Std. V to X.

Role-playing is not only interest-building but also a very powerful technique in which the students act out problems of human relations and analyse the enactment with the help of other role players and observers. Role-playing helps the pupils to get insights into their own problems as well as feelings, and it caters to the whole person as a learner.

Steps in the Role-Playing Process

The steps in the role playing process are —

1. Defining the Problem

The teacher here selects such a problem that is valid, meaningful and important to the group, and is concerned with human relations.

2. Establishing a Situation

After guessing the desired learning outcome, the teacher establishes a situation. It means this step is dependent on the desired learning outcome.

3. Casting of Characters

The teacher now selects only those pupils who can play the role well.

4. Briefing and Warming Up the Characters

The teacher helps the selected students to keep in mind the problem.

5. Acting

Students play their roles with action and dialogue.

6. Cutting

If it is found out by the teacher that the selected scene is getting longer, the role-play is cut short.

7. Discussion And Analysis

Now, the original problem under study is thrown to the students and reactions of the actors (behaviour aspect) as well as observers is discussed and analysed.

8. Summing Up

At this step, the teacher pins down whatever that has been learnt and helps the students to come to practical conclusion.

MAKING USE OF SLIDES OR FILMSTRIPS

Just like role-play, slide and film strips are also effective media for value-inculcation. In fact, its effectiveness is completely dependent on the tactfulness of the teacher.

Steps In The Usage Of Filmstrips Or Slides

The steps in the entire procedure of inculcating values through filmstrips or slides is as follows:

1. Review of filmstrips/slides

Before entering his or her class, the teacher uses the filmstrips or slides on a projector just to get familiar with the equipment that is going to be used in the class.

2. Script writing

Usually a commentary on the filmstrips or slides is prepared by the teacher in the form of a script.

3. Questions based on slides/filmstrips

The teacher writes few motivating questions on the board which becomes helpful for students to actively participate in the discussion.

4. Turning on the Projector

The teacher now starts the projector (which is already kept ready) and tells pupils to watch carefully. The teacher not only starts commenting, but if need be, certain slides are kept for a long time by the teacher.

5. Follow-up activity

The teacher now activates the class by leading pupils to answer to the questions already written on the board. Main emphasis here is to elicit from the pupils about what they have learnt from Slides/Filmstrips.

6. Goal-Setting

Here, pupils try to reflect what they saw and what changes have taken place in their minds. In fact, the teacher gets a feedback here for all the efforts put forth by him or her so far.

In the same manner, the inculcation of values is done by making use of the posters, Bulletin, Board, etc.

INCULCATION OF VALUES THROUGH DISCUSSION ON SLOGANS

The main purpose or objective here is to help students analyse a slogan and then apply it to one's own life by finding out the hidden values in the slogan.

The Slogans are either written on the blackboard by the teacher or a slip with at least five slogans printed is distributed among the students. Each slogan is taken for discussion one by one and students are asked to analyse each other's responses. Students are also asked to express their views as well as feelings and then are given encouragement for having dialogue in groups. The groups may be either of 10 students or at the most of 12 students.

The students then are asked to find out a subtle difference in between the slogans distributed among them. Then, they are also asked for a few questions as given below:

- Would you like to bring about any change in the given slogan?
- Out of the five slogans, arrange them prioritywise.
- What hidden values you could get from these slogans?
- How will you try to apply the hidden values from the slogan in your day-to-day life?

Lastly, the teacher leads the students to pray (prayer) and then asks them to disperse.

INCULCATION OF VALUES THROUGH GAMES

From the various types of curricular activities, games is another approach for the inculcation of values. The main purpose or objective here is to help students focus their attention on the values they cherish and also disclose the same to each other. The techniques made use of are Housie Games, Brainstorming and Discussion.

Now, before starting for the Housie Game, the students start with the prayer. Thereafter, the teacher explains the students about the Value Housie Game and then distributes the slips of Value Housie Game in the class. In all, 25 values are selected by the teacher and are written in each square of the slip distributed (instead of making use of numbers).

Equality of Gender	Punctuality	Sensitivity	Patriotism	National Integration
Courage	Dignity of Labour	Tidiness, Determination	Cleanliness, Love	Truthfulness, Co-operation

Slip of Value Housie Game

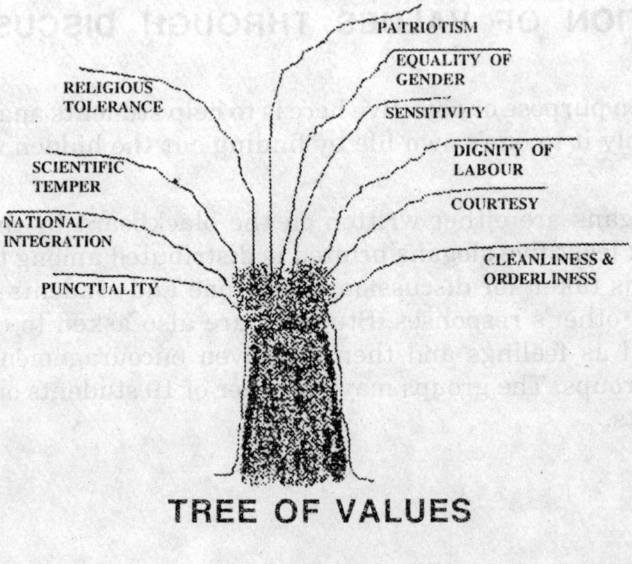

TREE OF VALUES

After having distributed Value Housie Game slips to all the students in the Class, the teacher instructs as follows:

"I hope each one of you is having a Value Housie Game Slip. Now I am going to call out the value. If you happen to find that value in one of the squares of your slip, put a cross (X) over the same. Suppose if all the squares of top-row has been filled out from your Value Housie Game Slip, then you are the winner. Then some amongst you may complete the middle row or a bottom row. Hence, when all the five squares of any row have been ticked/crossed by you, please stand up and announce."

The teacher is having 40 values, and after having declared the name of the winner, the teacher tells the students to read carefully all the 25 values from the squares of the slip of Value Housie Game Slip. The teacher now instructs them to make a list of these values in a prioritywise manner:

Viz. 1.

2.

3.

4.

The students arrange the values as per the importance given to each value by them. Thus, the most important comes on the top of the list and the least important goes to the bottom of the list.

The teacher now leads them for group discussion. Each group consists of 10 or 12 students. Here, in the group discussion, each student is made to tell as to why a particular value is at the top by him or her. Students thus reason.

Few questions as given below is then asked by the teacher —

- Did you like the game?
- Why?
- Which other game would you like to play this Value Housie Game? (Imagination, Creativity)
- What exactly have you learnt from this Value Housie Game?
- What changes would you like to bring about in this game?

The entire game then gets over with a prayer.

WAYS AND MEANS OF INCULCATING THE VALUES

It is felt that whatever has been discussed so far has given the idea regarding importing of values through curricular and cocurricular activities. However, it was sincerely felt that there should also be some more matter regarding approaches and techniques for the inculcation of ten values prescribed by Government of Maharashtra. Hence, the following discussion to give a clear cut idea to our readers.

I. Cleanliness and Orderliness

During school assemblies the focus may be put on the value of cleanliness once in a week as the rest of days in a week have to be kept for the inculcation of other values. Here, the teacher may use various types of aids like pictures, posters, slides, film strips. If this has to be done during assembly time, the teacher must make sure whether the space is sufficient.

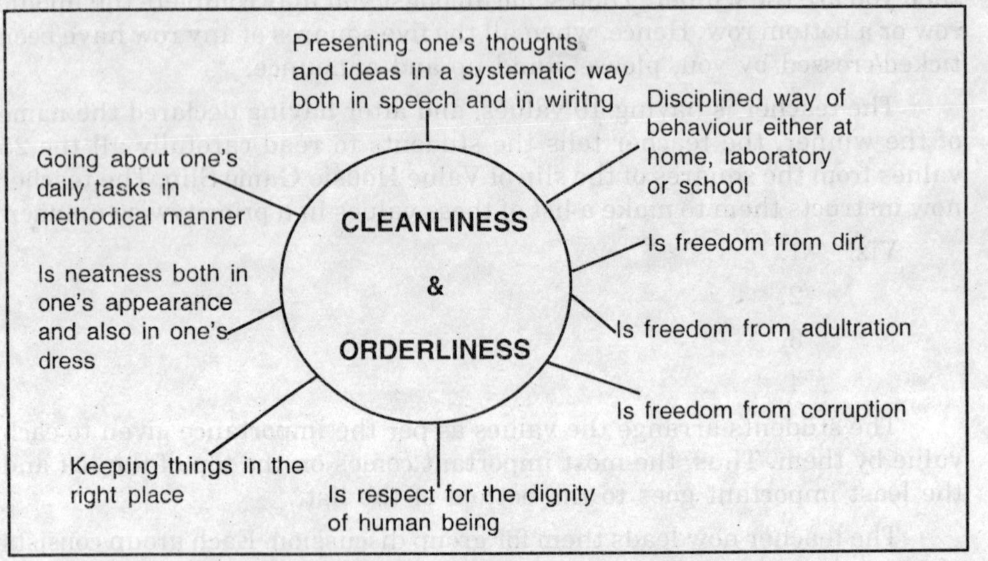

Further, if during school assemblies, it is not feasible to inculcate the value of cleanliness and orderliness as said above, the teacher may write certain important quotations and sayings as well as posters about cleanliness and display the same on the bulletin board.

At some other time, in actual periods, the teacher may read out poems based on cleanliness in the class and its theme may be discussed. Or, the teacher may even illustrate as many situations where the value of cleanliness is practised and where it is not practised.

Much of the discussion may run during science periods. So too, let there be cleanliness week once in a fortnight where pupils will be busy in cleaning their classes, floors, benches, etc.

II. Courtesy

This value can be inculcated by making it an integral part of each of the student in the class and almost in any period, viz., Language, History, Geography, Science. For instance, students may be told about good manners and etiquettes while talking to a friend, parent, teacher, neighbour etc. Let the students know that their voice should never be harsh. So too, particular words at a particular time, during the particular context have to be used viz. "Sorry", "Excuse me", "Thanking you", "Please", "I beg your pardon", etc. So also, occasionally, the teacher may bring it to the notice

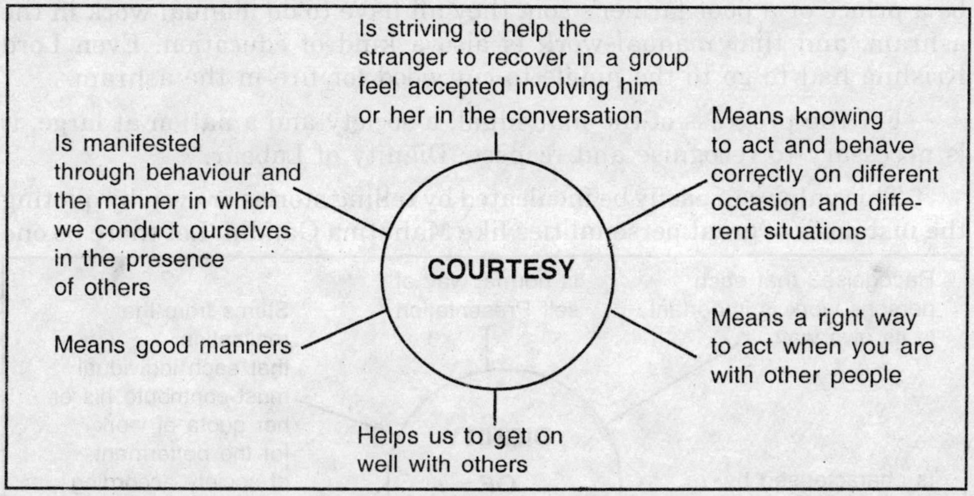

of the students about the manners while speaking on a telephone or while waiting in a queue. There should not be any act of disrespect on the part of the student. Many instances from stories in the text books during language period or even during history periods may be shown as an example to the students. They have also to be told of avoiding harsh talk or quarrelling, or loudly laughing or making the TV set on with full volume. Passport to popularity is a good smile on the face!

III. Dignity of Labour

His brow is met, with honest sweat,
He earns whatever he can,
And looks the whole world in the face,
For he owes not any man!!

By labour we generally mean manual work. Normally manual labour in our country is looked down upon, and the manual worker treated as an inferior being. Most of the ancient states were based upon slave-labour. Today's generation cannot survive without servants. More the number of servants richer is the person. Through value education we can tell children that instead of being stranded for want of some one else doing the work, it is always preferable to do that work ourselves as no work is small or big, dignified or undignified. We should never waste time by indulging in idleness, sluggishness and gossip. Instead we can utilise that time in cleaning our house, pressing our own clothes etc... which we think are the jobs of our servants!!

Thus, it sets an example for our children to be self-dependent and to respect labour and labourers. This is the only way to come up in life and prosper in the world.

In our ancient culture the schools were in remote places, where gurus needed to have ashrams. There, all students were treated equal. He could be a prince or a poor farmer's son, they all have to do manual work in the ashram, and that manual work is also a kind of education. Even Lord Krishna had to go to the jungle to cut wood for fire in the ashram.

For the progress of the individual, a society and a nation at large, it is necessary to recognise and respect "Dignity of Labour."

This value can easily be inculcated by telling stories or even by quoting the instances of great personalities like Mahatma Gandhi. Let there be one

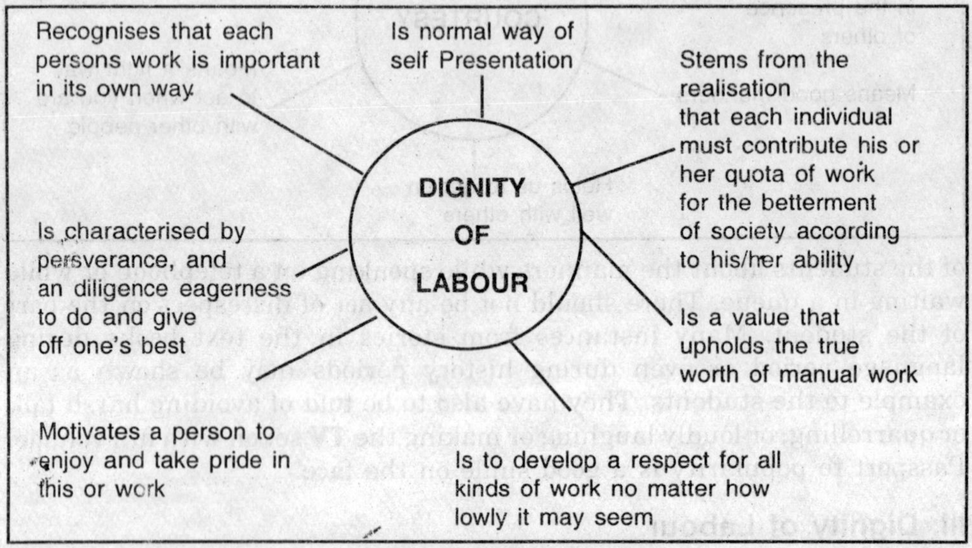

day in a fortnight where students will be asked to clean their classes, benches, floors, etc. So too different posters and pictures showing dignity of labour (that are available in the market) may be exhibited on the bulletin boards. Students from higher classes may be given a topic on dignity of labour and let there be a debate on the given topic. Or the students may be asked to write an essay or write a story pertaining to the value of dignity of labour.

IV. Equality of Sexes

Equal rights for men and women has been neglected even today!

Where women are respected, even gods lived there. In our ancient culture and during the Vedic period, women had more respect and status in society than man. No religious ceremony could performed by man alone, without the presence of his wife. Therefore, the Hindu male gods have the names of their consorts added before their own names. We say Sita Ram, Radha Krishna, Gauri Shankar, Laxmi Narayan and so on. The female is a better half of the male, without which the male cannot be complete.

We say, In the world of darkness and despair

Mind of men filled with fears.

Where men hope for morning to come.

In tired hearts, hopes have doomed.
Where all have to struggle to survive.
It is the woman who comes to revive!!

In some societies, women are treated as pieces of furniture whereas in some other societies, women are not considered as human beings! Though the Indian Constitution has given equal rights to women, due to blind faith, ignorance and misunderstanding, women are not able to exercise their fundamental rights.

Raja Ram Mohan Roy, Jyotiba Phule, Ramabai and Maharshi Karve are some of the prominent social reformers, who fought and work for the social freedom and welfare of the Indian women.

Today, we see women getting education and shouldering responsibilities of family, society and even the nation. But the percentage is very low. Yet the majority of women, especially in villages are uneducated and suppressed. The social activists are raising their voice through media against this injustice. But the corrupt politicians and the male-dominated social pattern do not allow their voices to be heard loud and clear.

Today's younger generation, through value education must be told that women can play an important role in reshaping the social, economic and political life of our country. Napoleon once said, "Give me good mothers and I will give you a good nation.

Thus, a country where women are suppressed, can never prosper and perhaps because of this, the future of India today is gloomy and uncertain!! The feeling of "it's never too late" should be inculcated in blooming buds, through value education.

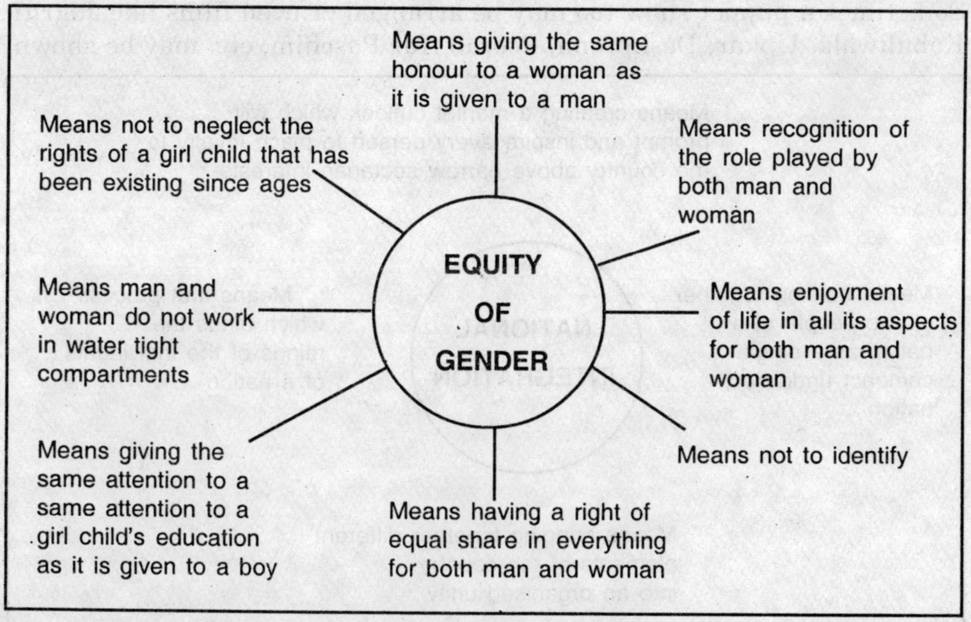

Particularly to the students of higher standard (Std. VIII, IX, X) the teacher may talk to them during assembly period on topics like 'Women in India', 'Status of Women — Yesterday and Today'. They may also be told about the struggle made for upliftment of women by great people like Mahatma Phule, Maharshi Karve, Raja Ram Mohan Roy, etc. Students may also be told about the need of equality of genders, in today's world. It should be very neatly and nicely brought out to the students that a man and a woman are actually substitutes for each other and they should never be looked at like two watertight compartments.

In recent times, even the judgements in the court are well-timed frames of references, which has to be told to the students of higher classes. Students must be made to understand about the rights of women and also right of education for a girl child.

Even in History period (as per the content) let the brave deeds of Rani of Jhansi, Sultana Razia, Ahilyabai Holkar, Chittur Chinnamma, etc. be described and explained how these great women fought shoulder to shoulder with men.

On occasions like Independence Day let the pupils be asked to write an essay on 'Gender Bias In Our Society' or let there be essay competition arranged in some standards of students as VIII A Vs. VIII B, etc.

V. National Integration

On the celebrations of days like Independence Day or Republic Day, let there be an address by the Headmaster or Principal of the school telling the significance of unity. In such speeches, certain quotations may be stated or some small story also may be told which will inspire the students. Sometimes a puppet show too may be arranged or even films like Jagriti, Kabuliwala, Upkar, Deshpremi, Poorab Aur Paschim, etc. may be shown.

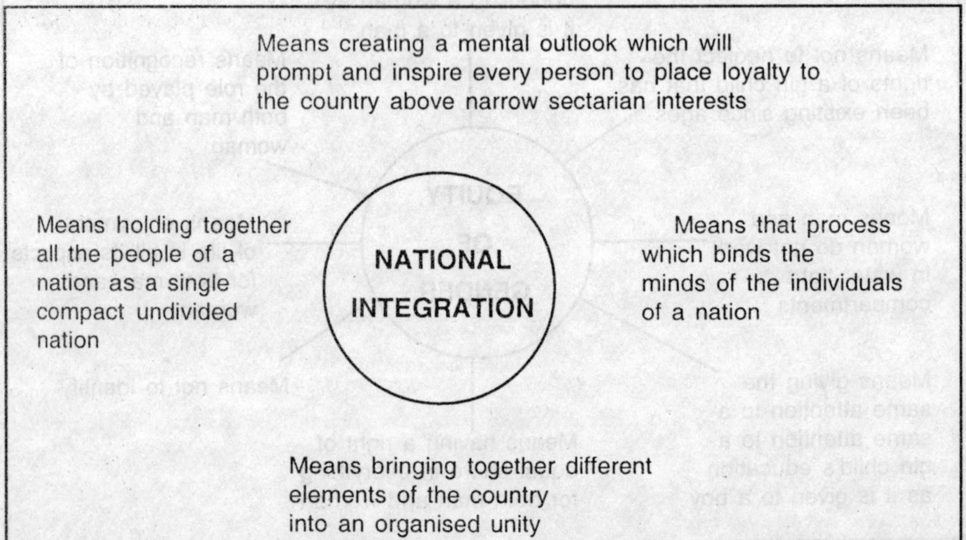

Barring aside these two important day celebrations, few ideas in the assembly periods may be brought out regarding the importance of unity. So too, occasionally, the students in a classwise manner may be asked to sing songs like 'Mile Sur Mera Tumhara, To Sur Bane Hamara'. Such things are not only thrilling but will be inspiring too to them. Through such activities, the students must be made to learn to share each other's joys, sorrow, smiles and tears as well and have common national ideal. They may even be asked to participate in essay competitions arranged by the school where the topics like "United We Stand, Divided We Fall" may be tackled. Organisation of exhibitions or educational trips may also be taken up as an additional activity to inculcate the value of National Integration.

VI. Patriotism

Means love for one's own motherland. Patriotism is the natural bond that unites a citizen to the country. We are born and brought up in our motherland and are nourished and nurtured by her.

She gives us food, clothes and shelter. Indeed! For everything we have, we are indebted to her. In short, India means Indian culture and civilisation. Our duty is to protect India and her rich cultural heritage. India is a melting point because nowhere in the world you will find such mixing of so many regions, religions and languages. To maintain peace, love and the above features one has to love and protect our national flag. The three colours of the flag i.e. saffron colour means supreme sacrifice white stands for 'peace' and green at the bottom symbolizes prosperity. The chakra stands for all round progress. Thus our flag has such indepth meaning that we should salute and proudly sing our national anthem as it is not merely a piece of cloth. After 15th August on 16th everywhere the flag is found in half torn conditions, peope just stamp on it and go. This should not happen. Moreover, a citizen must take interest in civic matters. Everyone should voluntarily vote. As the government provides facilities such as electricity, transport, roads, parks, water supply, flyovers, etc. All this costs money. Therefore, the contribution of citizens is very necessary, through payment of taxes. It is one thing to take legitimate advantage of the exemptions in the tax law, it is quite another matter to tell lies to distort and invest information while filing tax returns. A familiar excuse is, "everybody does it! here a person's honesty is at stake.This country's motto "satyameva jayate" truth shall prevail taken from Upanishads should be put in practice. Once values like, honesty, equality, religious tolerance etc. are present in each and every citizen then once again our motherland can become a "golden sparrow".

All these things are just in books. Nothing is seen in today's India. The people of India have become self-centered, backward, corrupt and politically ignorant. There is a crisis of character. Everybody wants to become a millionaire overnight by hook or crook. There is no communal harmony. In spite of these unhappy state of affairs, the situation can be controlled. India depends on her younger generations to free her once again from the shackles of her own corrupt and tyrant sons. The young men and women must come forward and wipe out the evils from our society. To achieve this, our education system must be overhauled. The youth of our country should be galvanized to safeguard India's integrity. Proper value education programmes should be conducted. Thus, we must act before it is too late.

Remembr, "Ask not, what your country has done for you, but ask what you have done for your country."

In the past, people like Mahatma Gandhi, Chandrashekhar Azad, Jawaharlal Nehru and others have sacrificed their life for their country. But today, if the situation arises where the students have to sacrifice their lives for their country, they will not do so. Not only this, they even find it difficult to show their loyalty by standing respectfully when the national anthem is sung. The need of today is to nurture the feeling of patriotism. The feeling of patriotism can be nurtured by collecting articles of patriotism and singing patriotic songs.

Today, there is very much need for the inculcation of this value. It should be brought to the notice of the students that patriotism does not mean just chanting the National Anthem or hoisting the National flag while celebrating national festivals; but it means a deep attachment and sincere pride to one's country. Hence, this values needs to be inculcated right from very early years.

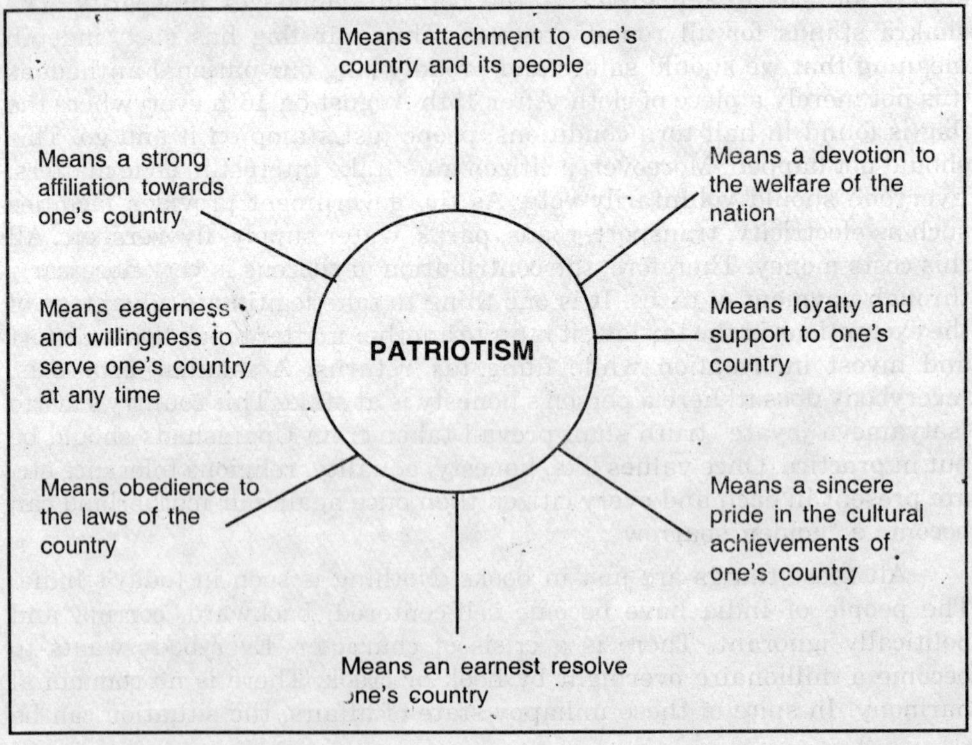

Anecdotes, posters, pictures of great National Leaders should be neatly exhibited on the celebrations of National festival days. Students must be initiated to sing songs like 'Ae Mere Vatan Ke Logo', 'Chalo Sipahi Chale', 'Mere Desh Ki Dharti', 'Hum Hindustani', 'Sare Jahan Se Achha', etc. Certain school assemblies may be arranged only on the topic of patriotism.

VII. Punctuality

Punctuality and discipline are the essential qualities of a fine character, because our character is the result of our conduct. "Punctuality is the key to success". In this connection we can say "early to bed and early to rise makes a man healthy, wealthy and wise!" Through value education children should be told the importance of punctuality. Any work done regularly always achieves its results. For example, when students are writing their papers in the examination hall, if they do not finish writing in the allotted time, then whatever they have learnt becomes useless. The smallest work done in time proves to be a great asset in life.

The teacher has to quote many instances about the importance of punctuality varieties of things like pictures, posters, quotations etc. may be made use of by the teacher. It will be still more beneficial if the proverbs and quotations regarding punctuality are shown through slides. The importance of doing all the things at a particular time to be explained to the students by the teacher. Punctuality is that value which can be

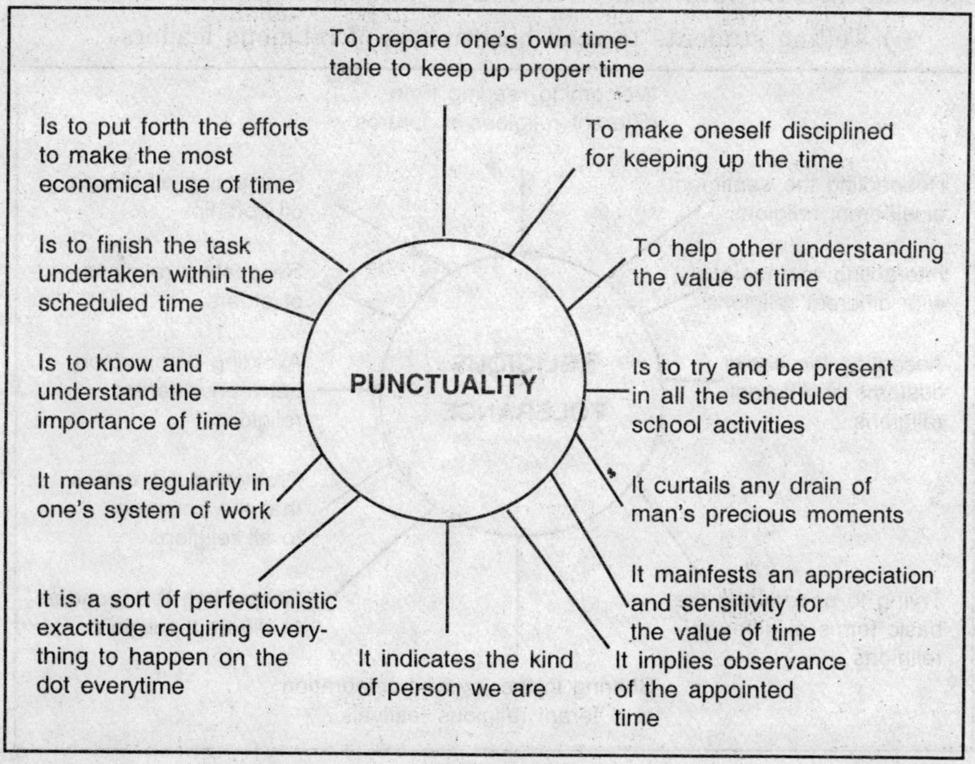

	STATEMENTS	A	B	C	D	E
1.	I go to school on time					
2.	I keep up the appointments					
3.	I always return on time the things that I Borrow					
4.	I waste my time by watching TV					
5.	Etc.					
6.	Etc.					

inculcated by giving the students Self-Evaluation Sheet, containing certain statements for rating and students must be told to do the rating with honesty and truthfulness (which are also important values). For example, certain statements as given below may be given with key — Always (*A*), Often (*B*), Sometimes (*C*), Seldom (*D*), Never (*E*). Put a tick mark in the columns which is honestly felt to be true to your conscience.

Even here also, the students may be asked to write essays on topics like "Time is Lost, Everything is Lost". Such pupils may even be selected for essay writing competitions.

VIII. Religious Tolerance

This value is to be inculcated in our students right from their tender age, and the said value can be inculcated through various means like —

(*i*) Telling students to read biographies of religious leaders.

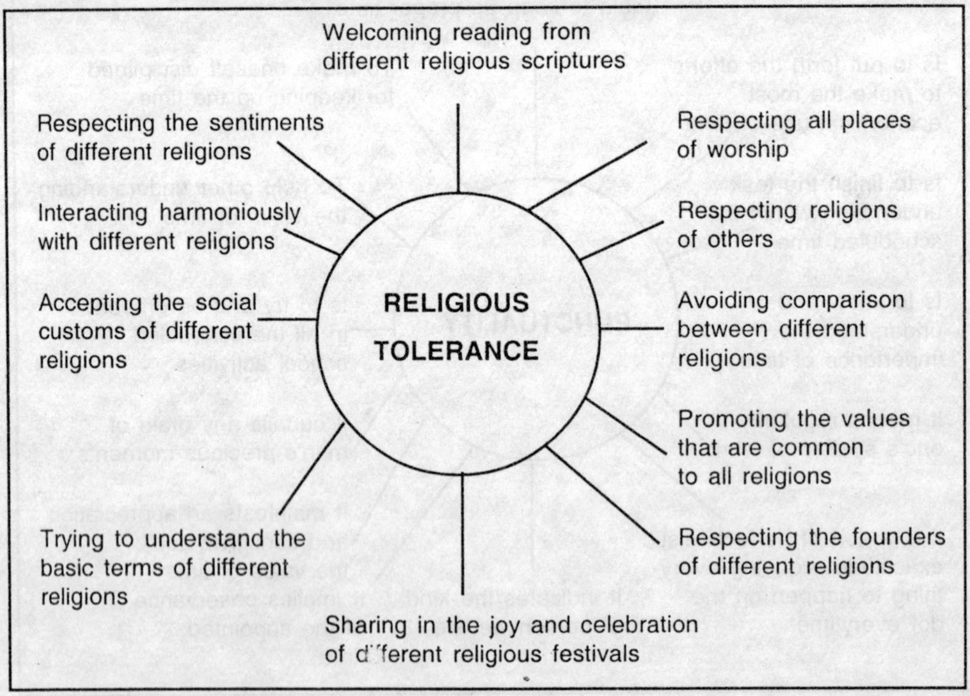

(ii) Teacher to tell the real life stories about religious leaders.

(iii) Particularly on days like Parsee New Year Day, Gudhi Padva Day, etc., posters and pictures reflecting the value may be exhibited in school.

(iv) On such occasions, films like Mustafa, Krantiveer, etc. may be shown to children.

(v) Based on the text (certain lesson from language text books or topics from History), the activity of role-play or dramatisation may be arranged by the teacher.

(vi) And, on certain important festivals like Diwali, X-mas, Pateti, etc. let the students from different religions participate in assemblies that are carefully organised in schools.

IX. Scientific Temper

Most important thing is to make our students realise the fact that one should not accept anything blindly. Particularly in science periods (pertaining to topic), the teacher may again and again try to inculcate this in the unripe minds. This will help students to observe things very minutely. The children will also come to know the importance of hygiene. Even in a Geography period, the students will be made to understand how things happen at a particular time in a particular manner e.g. during the month of Shravana, Hindus do not eat non-vegetarian food, because month of Shravan falls in monsoon season and during monsoon, food that is difficult to digest should be avoided. This must be specifically made known to the students. So too, underground stems like garlic, ginger etc. are not eaten during monsoon because of the slush in which the grow at this time.

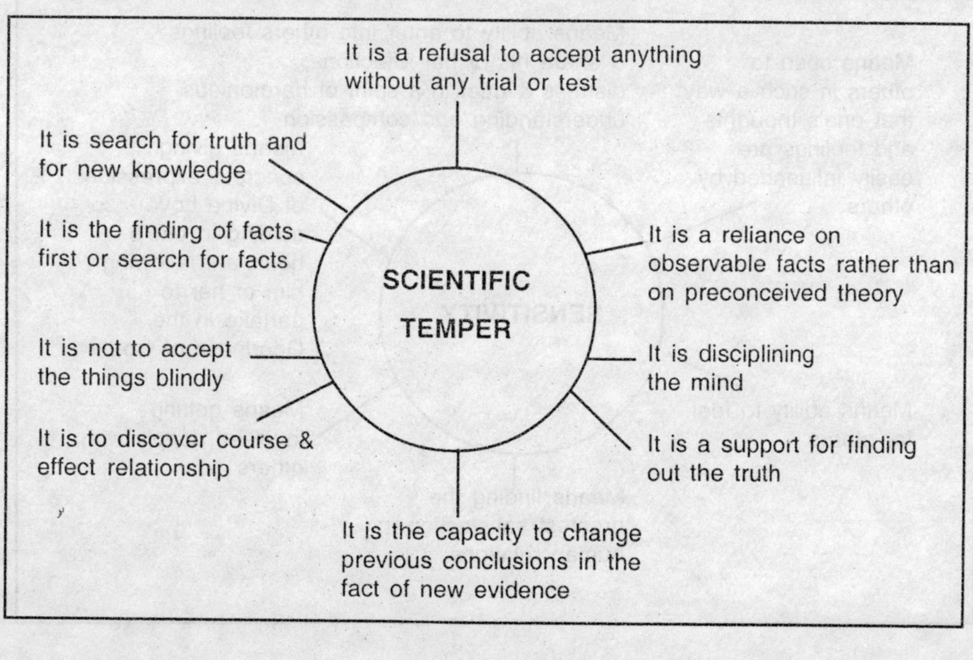

It is essential for schools to arrange science exhibitions where the student must be asked to prepare models, charts, apparatus, etc. Further, debate on subject of science with topics like — "Science A Blessing. Not A Curse" may be arranged.

As said earlier, students should not be allowed to accept things blindly, particularly when they have misconcepts regarding the disease like leprosy. Hence, a fair and clearn talk may be arranged by living experts who will not only remove the misconcepts but will also give a correct information about the harmful results or consequences of diseases like AIDS. This is very important.

So also, we all know SUPW is an important activity of the school. It is here, students may be asked to prepare soap, chalks, etc. which gives them knowledge of dignity of labour, joy of cooperation, rise in curiosity and developing the attitude of self-help.

A proper guideline to pupils regarding the value of scientific temper will definitely develop good habits in them like washing hands before meals, watching TV from a proper distance, performing experiments in an orderly manner, continue reading the book when there is enough light in the room, etc.

X. Sensitivity.

The ability to enter into others' feelings in sensitivity and this is expressed through —

Sensitivity to one's family.

Sensitivity to one's society.

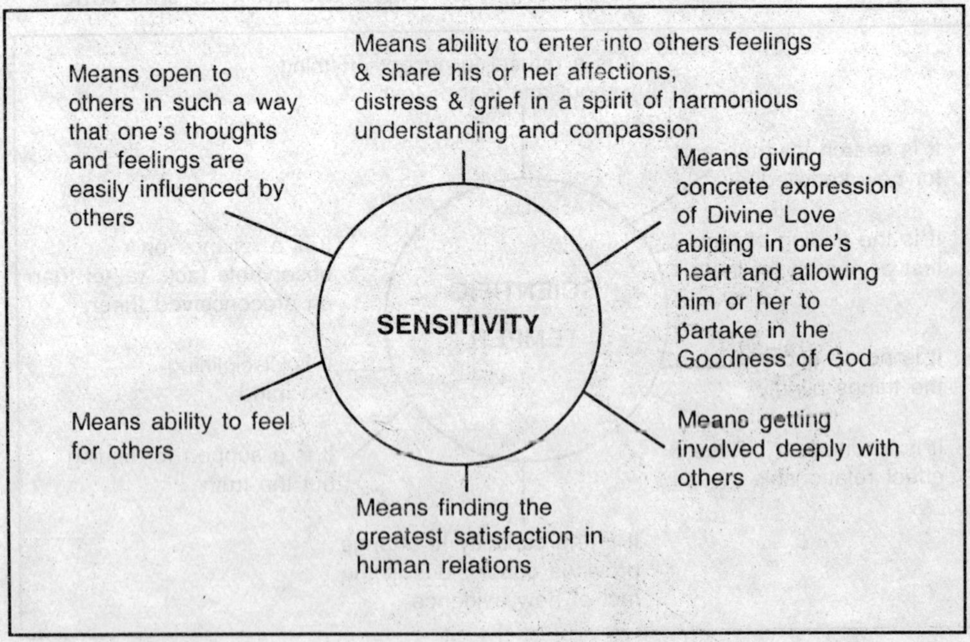

Sensitivity to one's environment and

Sensitivity to the world at large.

This value can be exercised

(*i*) By telling stories.

(*ii*) By exhibiting pictures, posters and cartoons.

(*iii*) By reading our good poems to students.

(*iv*) By making children listen to recorded songs.

(*v*) By writing a script and asking pupils to dramatize.

(*vi*) By clipping few quotations and sayings on the board viz.

- One should be generous to all creations.
- As you would not harm yourself, you should not harm others.
- You must help those who are in need.
- Charity without fellow feeling is like showing a fallow land.

For all the explained exercises for inculcation of values among the students, it is the teacher first of all, who has to be honest and sincere in trying to shape the pupils for their all-round development. In this connection, it is better to quote the following poem:

If you wish
To put yourself
In a correct gear
Then, please try
To change atmosphere
By enhancing love and care
Do not forget
That all are Divine
With innumerable
Potentialities underlying
World will be
Always with you
When you give respect
And never, never
Feel yourself as
"Always the Best"

CONCLUDING REMARKS

It should be brought clearly here that educational institutions alone cannot combat all the social or emotional prejudices and intellctual errors prevailing in the society. Other social organisations or institutions also should strive to rehabilitate the basic values further and it is essential to create a reward structure for good conduct and it constitutes the best motivation for the acquisition of values.

It is also to be noted that there are ways and means for inculcating values in our children. It is not possible to enumerate and discuss all of them in detail. This current chapter is intended to trace in brief, the suggested approaches and to find out some other ways and means and then suggest measures of teaching values in our Indian schools. One thing to be brought out to our readers is that teaching of values is necessary for remedying many ills that our world of education and our society as a whole is suffering.

One should also be aware of the fact that it is the classroom that sends the message of love, security, belongingness, warmth. It is the message, where each each pupil is respected and trusted and made to be engaged in such activity where, learning and living are united. Hence, let our children be provided with opportunities to live in our classrooms like perfect human beings. The informal and effective participation of the students with each other in every sphere of education is needed if humanity is to survive and meet the challenges of the future.

So too, let us not forget the instructive short story given by Gurudev Rabindranath Tagore entitled "THE PARROT'S TRAINING". The moral of the story is that whatever structures we may build for education, whatever facilities we may create for students and teachers, nothing will be of any real use if we forget that education should subserve the highest interest of the child in a system that would imprison its free and living movements and if we stuff the child with the plethora of materials the child will get suffocated and may even wither away.

Let us, therefore, create for our children such nurseries where they can blossom like smiling and shining flowers spreading their fragrance by their vibrating freshness and youthfulness.

THIS SHALL BE THE SOUL FOR EDUCATION!

MAINTAINING A RECORD

Now, comes a question of how to evaluate as well as how to keep a record of each pupil. What should the teacher do? OR What exactly is expected of the teacher in knowing how his or her pupils have not only understood the importance of values but how are they implementing the same. There are very many ways and means. However, finding the following method to be more suitable for using, the things are stated as below:

VALUE EDUCATION (STD. V TO X)

Scheme of marks to be allotted to each value.

I.	**Patriotism**	
1.	Writes patriotic poems and learns them by heart	2
2.	Says National Anthem and pledge properly — Respect them.	2
3.	Presents patriotic songs and dialogues with acting	2
4.	Uses lights, fans etc. in the class properly. Takes care that water is not wasted.	2
5.	Takes care that public places don't get dirty e.g. school walls, passages, toilets, bus stands....	2
		10
II.	**National Integration**	
1.	Learn by heart Maharashtra Geet and songs on National Integration	2
2.	Collects information about customs and mannerism of different states	2
3.	Collects information about the ceremonies and festivals of other states.	2
4.	Helps and sympathises fellow countrymen affected by natural calamities.	2
5.	Is proud of the games, players and literature, geographical peculiarities of other states.	2
		10
III.	**Religious Tolerance**	
1.	Writes down the names of reference books and places of worship devotion to all religions	2
2.	Learn by heart different religious prayers	2
3.	Narrates and writes information about saints and founders from different religions	2
4.	Collects preaching of saints of different religions	2
5.	Participates in religious festivals other than his own	2
		10
IV.	**Equality of Gender**	
1.	Is friendly towards both boys and girls in school	2
2.	Does clearning work at home and school	2

3.	Does things on his/her own. Does not depend on mother/father, sister/brother.	2
4.	Gathers knowledge about the laws for upliftment of women	2
5.	Reads autobiographies of capable women and understands their contribution	2
		10

IV. Dignity of Labour

1.	Sweeps the class and keeps it clean.	2
2.	Collects labourer's songs.	2
3.	Participates in cleanliness drive for school, surroundings.	2
4.	Collects information about labourers and sympathises with them	2
5.	Participates in "Shramdhan" camps	2
		10

VI. Scientific Temper

1.	Prepares scientific instruments and collects scientific pictures.	2
2.	Participates in Science Exhibition/reads scientific stories.	2
3.	Collects information about scientists and narrates them.	2
4.	Collects information with diagrams for machines, factories' electrical instruments.	2
5.	Utilises national wealth such as electricity, water, fuels and with care. Participates in tree plantation and Environment day.	2
		10

VII. Modesty

1.	Behaves politely with all teachers, servants and friends.	2
2.	Speaks politely to Parents, Teachers, Elders.	2
3.	Apologises for mistakes	2
4.	Conscious of rules, regulations, conventions and traditions of the institutions.	2
5.	Gives due weightage to other opinions while acting rightly.	2
		10

VIII. Sensitivity

1.	Does not pluck flowers from gardens in school or public gardens.	2
2.	Renders help during natural/national calamities.	2
3.	Collects poems which depicts violence.	2
4.	Writes about the work "Rutuchakra".	2
5.	Helps the needy students of the class.	2
		10

IX. Punctuality/Time Management

1.	Punctual in coming to school.	2
2.	Punctual in attending Value Education and Prayer-Classes	2
3.	Completes the assigned work without delay	2
4.	Punctual in attending all cocurricular activities	2
5.	Apologises if not punctual.	2
		10

X. Orderliness-Neatness

1.	Keeps the uniform neat	2
2.	Covers the Text books/Notebooks properly	2
3.	Answers all the question papers very neatly	2
4.	Behaves properly in all the programmes	2
5.	Collects good thoughts and stories	2
		10

NAME OF TEACHER ____________ STD. ________ DIV. ______ YEAR ________

Sr. No. Name of the Student	Semester	Patriotism	National Integration	Religious tolerance	Equalityo of Gender	Dignity of Labour	Scientific Attitude	Modesty	Sensitivity	Time Management/ Punctuality	Orderliness/ Neatness	Total	Average	Grade
		10	10	10	10	10	10	10	10	10	10	10		
		1												
		2												
		1												
		2												
		1												
		2												
		1												
		2												
		1												
		2												
		1												
		2												
		1												
		2												
		1												
		2												
		1												
		2												
		1												
		2												

VALUE EDUCATION: A MISSING LINK IN HIGHER EDUCATION

13

Materialism, power, ego, corruption and selfishness are the leading factors upon humanism. Eagerness for unjustified wealth, insensitivity, gross injustice of human rights and unhealthy competition has become the only spirit of all the giants of the society. In present life there is crisis of values and idealogies in every walk of life. The weakening of eternal values in the younger generation have caused many serious problems. As a human being, one must have a knowledge of uiversal values. In fact, a human being and values are inseperable. Hence, for proper human values one must develop a sense of national unity and integrity. Now, National unity does not mean political unity. It is much higher than this. Because, it includes the thoughts and sentiments of its citizens which govern their sum total of behaviour. In fact, countless evils in our society has disturbed our day-to-day living.

Various barbaric qualities and other destructive forces give clear indication of the process of degeneration of human society. True to say that communication is the key factor in inculcating values. There is a need to understand the attitudes, emotions, feelings and motives of pupils. Hence, the importance of value-educations in the educational institutions. No doubt, values can be transmitted through action; yet communication seem to be the most important. In many institutions, curriculum of value education is formal and direct; while in large number of schools it is informal and indirect. In fact, learning of values cannot be restricted to classroom instructions alone. Hence, the schools must take into cognizance all types of social influences affecting the development of values in pupils. Values get transmitted via both the implicit and planned curriculum.

What has been said so far, the point emphasized is that the entire process of value education is a highly comprehensive and complex one that involves a wide range and variety of learning experiences. All forms of learning cannot be provided though single source or teacher should draw from a variety of learning resources either independently or in combination.

Academic institutions in India were Gurukulas for centuries where the Gurus gave the students a *multi-dimensional* man-making education; such education co-ordinated well the three *Hs of the learners. HEAD, HEART* and *HAND,* i.e., it took care of the intellectual and emotional growth of the students and the development of their skills. The Gurus believed that education is a process in Gurukulas where the students are developed in to respectable citizens. They taught the students values, which guided them to a healthy and harmonious social life; *the Gurus believed that human values are what the students should live by and what they would die for.* The Gurus were convinced that providing with the students the knowledge and skills that would enable them to realise their professional aspirations is only part of their education; the more important part was making them young citizens of *values, culture* and *patriotism.* They prepared the students to face the challenges of career and life by inculcating in them values and developing in them a positive attitude; the values and the right attitude helped their own progress and the progress of their society. *To put it in nutshell education in ancient Indian was not mere imparting* of knowledge and teaching of skills. It was, on the contrary, a mission for man-making.

The popular concept of modern day education, particularly higher education, has changed adversely. The objectives seem to be coaching the students for passing the university examination with good marks and giving them a few vocational skills to fit them in to a job. In the man-making education head saw the meaning of information, heart saw its righteousness and use within the boundaries of morality and hand put it into action. But the modern higher education has ignored the heart; it has ignored the fact that students are a subject matter of immense significance both for the present and the future of their country. The higher education in Science and Technology, which, majority of the students opt for tries to equip them for materialistic development, which is mistaken to 'progress'. The engineers, doctors, scientists, economists and men of commerce change very much in the name of civilization and they advance materialistically but they do not 'progress'. Change and materialistic development do not signify human progress and the progress of the society. Again there is a limit for the human to absorb changes and materialistic development. The present day youth stretch themselves beyond the limits to the extent of disturbing their mental poise and affecting the psychological well-being. The values are forsaken and the interpersonal relationships are breaking down. The youth have become the victims of over vaulting materialistic ambition and unknowingly have accelerated the pace of their life. They are not able to slow down now. The result is gastrics, neurosis, mental disorder and behavioural problems. The youth have been caught in 'achievement fever' and have become slaves of their own machines. Few Yogi exercises will definitely show the positive effect — but our edu-system has not taken any cognisence of it. The higher educational is teaching the youth to live by machines and gadgets, not by the universal human values like truth, non-violence, love and compassion. These values are relegated and man is fast becoming a non-entity. The young men want to be always busy about their business and industry which can multiply their money. Leisure and social get-together are considered a sin. Their diaries are jam packed with their programmes and their phones melt in their hot breath. The result is obvious. The family and the society are breaking away. When the values are forsaken chaos overtakes order. The present way of thinking, behaviour and life is changing so adversely that there is now an urgency to make value education an integral part of higher education. Machines like computer and information systems like internet have so advanced that we cannot wait any longer for any natural process to redeem the youth from the commercialised way of functioning and artificial way of living. Life has become so artificial and materialistic that the young men and women have begun to think whether they need any value system at all that will guide them to the right way of living. If this doubt becomes a conviction life will not be human and our society cannot be called a humane society. Once upon a time it was heard the husband and wife saying to each other "I cannot live without you". Today it is the other way — "I cannot live with you!"

The fast life and madness for money have been badly mistaken for 'progress' and the youth are already in the grip of a frenzy for such a kind of progress. The result is, as has already been said, trembling fingers, rumbling stomachs and fast beating hearts. They ar obsessed with such 'progress' that they do not know what to speak to others, and what they can give to others. There is always a sense of urgency with everybody. They are tense even when they do not anything; they are tense perhaps they are worried they are not doing anything in that particular hour. Impatience is becoming the ruling principle and men and women want to work even when they are physically exhausted. They are particular to keep themselves busy even when it is unnecessary. They think it is below their dignity to take the company of men who work slowly and leisurely.

How has it all happened? It has all happened because life has been mistaken to be a synonym for technical expertise of technical know-how. 'The knows' in a frenzy to accumulate materialistic wealth try to exploit 'the know nots'. There is an awakening among the youth now about this exploitation and there is an aggression on both sides. The general awakening and the resultant anxiety have lead to unhealthy competition in the academic world, cut-throatism in business world and crimes and violence in political world. Integrity in character, public manners and social controls are breaking down. *Life has become a rat race and completing the tasks before the deadline has become the ruling phrase. Man is looked at as a multi-functioning machine, not as a valuable organic being. There is always a tension between man and his time as he wants to make the most prosperity out of it. The results are stress and anxiety and breakdown of health.*

There are of course the more alarming consequences. Materialistic development and crimes have begun to grow together. Technology goes handy to the criminals and often we read in the newspapers about *high tech-cheating, high tech-forgery* and *hightech-serial killing.* The youth live in a country where hatred grows in the name of religion, crimes in the name of politics and violence in the name of nationalism. Separatist forces try to give refuge to the unemployed but aggressive youth. The real patriot is becoming an alien in his own motherland.

Ours is a land of Buddha and Mahatma Gandhi, and it is supposed to be a land of truth and non-violence, but as Dalai Lama once observed, much of non-violence has been exported to other countries, and there is violence here. Politicians think that they are a class above the common man and play havoc. *For many politicians lie is the key weapon for their survival.* It happened that a bus full of politicians was going at a high speed. Suddenly it lost its control, nose dived in to a field and crashed into trees. The farmer, the owner of the field dug a hole and buried all the politicians. The police officer who went to investigate the accident asked the farmer, "Were you sure all of them were dead?" The farmer replied, "I remember some of them said they were alive but we know how politicians always tell lies." Our politicians talk so much about the character of the nation that they forget their own. What is worse some of the members of Legislature in a few states are confirmed criminals. The proportion of criminals is increasing from election to election.

Times are hard for the student community of our country and the policy makers for higher education have an urgent task of redeeming the youth from the hell fire of commercialised education (here the reference is particularly to self-financing institutions) and the mechanical academic life.

Before a programme of value education in higher education is presented here, it is worth, it is felt that the five salient features of 1988 Youth Policy are quoted here. The policy unfortunately did not take off, but the objectives have been well thought out and written. The five objectives the policy came out with are:

1. to instill in the youth a deep awaremess and a respect for the principles enshrined in the constitution, and willingness to further the rule of law with commitment to national identity, integration, non-violence, secularism, and socialism.

2. to promote awareness of the cultural heritage with a commitment to their prerservation as well as the enrichment of their environmental and ecology.

3. to develop qualities of discipline, self-reliance, justice and fair play, sporting spirit, concern for public welfare, and scientific temper to combat superstition, obscurantism, and such social evils.
4. to provide maximum access to education for personality development as well as vocational training; and
5. to make youth aware of international issues and to involve them in promoting peace, understanding a just economic order.

This paper wants to highlight the third and the fourth objectives here as they are very important to the present day higher education. There should be at least one session a week for value education in higher education. The students can be divided into groups for classes on Personality Development. *Teaching and practice of Meditation and Yoga, Democratic thinking, Inter religious dialogue, Communication skills and Group Discussion* on current affairs can be part of the programme for value education. 1988 Youth Policy says that the youth of India have "a right as well as an obligation to participate actively in the national deveopment and shaping the destiny of the nation". The youth cannot shape the destiny of their nation without the value education to them. The aim of value education in higher education is obvious, it is to enable the youth to become admirable young men, men of scientific temper and human spirit, men deeply patriotic men who can rise above the deceptive propaganda of many politicians and separatist forces.

Yoga and meditation discipline the five senses, and allow the reason work as they control the emotions. They help the students to affirm the facts and choose their activities. They develop in them an ability to act with freedom and confidence. Inter religious dialogue is the need of the hour. The youth should know that religion is for man and man is not be religion. The ultimate purpose of any religion can be to elevate man to the state of a saint. If any religion breeds hatred it cannot be religion at all.

Communication skills prove to be an important tool for the youth to absorb value education and conduct programmes on it in and out the college premises. Efficient communication is not a born gift like talent in music or painting. It is an art cultivated over a period of years. The students should first start with dialogue, proceed to group discussion and end with debate and public speaking. While group discussion socializes every participant, debate and public speaking make him a leader.

Meditation *sharpens the intellect of a student.* Gyles Brandreth comments on debate thus: "For the inexperienced and nervous speaker, one of the best ways of learning the art of public speaking and conquering fear is to take part in debate. Debating encourages quick thinking and gives valuable practice in putting thoughts into words in front of an audience.

Again as Joseph Joubert says the aim of argument, or of discussion, should not be victory, but progress. Debate teaches the participants self-discipline and it helps them to discover their merits and inadequacies.

So too, successful teachers teaching Yogic Exercises must be invited to conduct the workshops. However, right guidance and continuous practice is a must.

The campuses should take classes and conduct workshops for the students on this art. The youth should know how this art turned to be a great asset to leaders like Lincoln, Churchil, John F. Kennedy and Jawaharlal Nehru. But it cannot be acquired overnight. One of the successful executives who attended a Talk-Power seminar organised by Natalie Rogers confessed, "I just go into a state of shock when I have to address a group. Last year I was supposed to make an honorary presentation at a dinner, and I had to bow out at the last minute. My knees were shaking so badly I couldn't walk. I can't tell you how embarrassing it was." *It needs right guidance and continuous practice; patient practice can make public speaking,* which may otherwise look a mysterious art, a possible skill.

Group Discussion, Debates and practice sessions of Public Speaking should be conducted in the campuses on the erosion caused to values in modern day life. These great arts of communication teach the youth first discipline, as discipline is doing something which does not come esasily. It is the practice of chosen profession with commitment and conscience that can make somebody excel in it. A disciplined person is not a rigid person. He is one who takes care of his self and development. He knows discipline is forming right habits for a harmonious living, it is not self negation. Activities like the above give the youth opportunity to be disciplined, to develop their personality and to develop their capability to function as admirable young men. Equal attention should be given to activitiers like verse writing, story writing and dialogue writing on themes of human values — importance of prayer, yoga exercise and over and above meditation.

It is these activities on value education that teach the youth the principle that personal integrity is more important than company manners. It is the value education that gives their life a concrete direction, meaning and profundity. The values shape their inner sense of what is right and what is wrong. Values are not laws but they are principles that show a person who he is. It is in the light of values the youth should make the hard choices in life. When they make the right choice, they should act with integrity, honesty, courage and generosity.

The value education teaches the youth that knowledge and skill are not the only requisite to succeed in life, but a positive attitude and human way of action. The values teach the youth to laugh at their miseries and be sad at others' miseries. Men with values and independent thinking do not succumb to pressure from time and from their competitors. They follow their own beliefs and mode of action. It is the person who succeeds in the right way is the one who inspires others to succeed.

Value education from the perspective of the student also sheds important light on character education. To effectively teach character education, teacher must follow the rules and show respect for all students. "Do as I say, not as I do" definitely does not work. It is said that model teachers earn respect by being fair, genuine, hard-working, caring and good listeners. Students believe that what a teacher does is more important than what a teacher says. To them actions clearly speak louder than words.

Integration of character education into all courses and by teaching values through the invisible curriculum, we can avoid the divisiveness usually associated with specific character education programmes. The following strategies are recommended for teachers for teaching value education:

1. Educating the whole person by focussing on student knowledge, behaviour and feeling.
2. Choosing content that honours and rewards virtue in examples, and encouraging reflection on values content.
3. Using quotes, pledges, sincerely with high expectation for all students codes, and guidelines.
4. Communicating clearly, consistently.
5. Developing student skills in resisting peer pressure, maintaining self-respect, and resolving conflicts in non-violence ways.
6. Being a good role model through positive personal example.
7. Using and requiring respectful language.
8. Using the creation of and even-handed enforcement of just classroom rules to teach core values.
9. Reinforcing the diligent work and virtuous behaviour of students with praise and appreciation.
10. Correcting unethical, immoral and disrespectful behaviour or become an 'enabler.'
11. Having students work together co-operatively in heterogeneous groups.
12. Involving peers, parents and community.
13. Encouraging students involvement in community service and
14. Teaching not preaching.

The value education is targeted at elementary level because it is widely recognised that values are learned at a very young age and the basic personality of the child is formed at the age of 3 to 4 years. Some children come to school with this values well established but the environment around them helps to modify these values as they mature. These values, which are modified throughout life, become more resistant to change.

Most of the value education programmes are concentrated at the elementary level even though most irresponsible acts are committed by adolescents and by adults. Psychiatrist William Glasser (1965), author of "Reality Therapy" insist that it is never too late to teach values which strengthen character.

CONCLUDING REMARKS

Value education is education in values and education towards the inculcation of values. And the core idea behind value education is to cultivate essential values in the students so that the civilization that teaches us to manage complexities can be sustained and further developed. Value education is a universal phenomenon intrinsic to all learning and education, whether at home or in an institution. It is not. Neither teaches to be critical thinkers or to regard ourselves as proactive beings in relation to ourselves, community and humanity at large. Unwittingly and through habit, one accepts most things handed out to us by the media, the government and the polity. Unfortunately when there is so much talk about individual capabilities and potentialities, there is so little confidence on the part of the individual about his own power to make a difference. Since the students are not trained to be proactive thinkers because they are told so little of the life values that is the basis for creative thinking. It is up to us, educationist to determine the society we will create by deciding upon the values we will emphasise in value education.

New generations are having different type of challenges to face. For that they have to accept different convictions and prove themselves to be fittest. Today, the education imparted to our children is almost solely limited to 'education for bread and butter'. Students are led to believe that by developing the ability to gather, store, and retrieve vast information, they stand educated. But Swami Vivekananda points out, "Education is not the amount of information that is put into your brain and runs riot there, undigested all your life. We must have life-building, man-making and character-making assimilation of ideas." Mere academic knowledge without deep rooting in moral and spiritual values will only fashion lop-sided personalities who may become rich in material possessions, but will remain poor in self-understanding, peace, "The wise man built his house upon the rock, The foolish man built his upon the sands, Then came the waves and washed the sands away, but the house upon the rock did not even sway". Values are virtues, ideals and qualities on which actions and beliefs are based, guiding principles that shape individuals, outlook, attitudes and conduct. Values in education have been visualised at a national level initiative to sensitize parents, teachers, teacher educators, educational administrators, policy makers and community agencies, etc. for promotion of value oriented education. The focus is on generating awareness, material develpment, teachers training, promotion of research and innovation in the area of education of human values development of guidelines for value education in the school system. The development of human values aims to develop the individual as 'self'. Which is also the ultimate aim of education and it is directly an attempt towards human learning. The National Curriculum Framework (2005) has highlighted the values of democracy, equality, justice, freedom and concern for others' well-being, secularism, respect for human dignity and rights as providing perspective to the goal of education. Development of human values focused on guiding the student to be an agent of positive change for transformation of society. It does not aim at adding a new subject or separate activity rather an integration of peace perspective, attitude and values in the entire school climate, the curricular activities and interactions in and out the classroom among teachers and pupils.

Lastly, it may be concluded by saying that a family that prays together and dines together, stay together!

14

VALUE-EDUCATION: ITS PSYCHOLOGICAL PARAMETERS

In fact, it is through the educational processes that value-education tries to develop different behavioural patterns; and it is through these patters of behaviour, the pupil conceives values in terms of acceptable human requirements. It is because of such things that values are broadly termed as code of conducts or set of behaviour which brings harmony, happiness and progress in the set of systems as family, community and society. It is here that one gets the guidance of right or wrong doing as well as good or evil.

On the basis of the above said facts along with educatonists, psychologists too consider value-inculcation in terms of behaviour pattern which can be explained on the basis of theories and models of behaviours. Hence, they generally avoid the question of value-education although, they suggest that erosion of values in the behaviour of a pupil causes psychological break-down and he or she shows symptoms of all sort of depression — viz., frustration, insecurity, loneliness, etc., and, even sometimes drug addiction, deliquency, etc.

It is the social stability of the pupil which depends on his or her value-systems and moral development. In the very early stages of schooling, it is really very difficult for a pupil to understand the values of moral behaviour but soon he or she tries to identify the difference between right and wrong doing. In fact, such a knowledge the pupil receives at home as well as in school. When something goes wrong by him or her; there comes a feeling of guilt which is easily seen by his or her overt behaviour (feeling of shame) and it is at this juncture, a readiness is seen in him or her to rectify the errors and then control wrong doings by putting the efforts in the right direction of action. However, in the absence of proper guidelines or attention by elders (teachers or parents) he or she, later on, does not even try to improve his or her behaviour. Not only this, but he or she does not even show any guilt feeling in his or her overt behaviour too. As such, human mind is too clever to always find out suitable arguments to cover his or her guilt and also explain what he or she does not want to do!

From the above said facts it goes without saying that value-education must start from the very beginning. It is at a very young age, the child starts getting some knowledge regarding the social norms of the society. Therefore, it is very essential that a teacher should have a sound psychological knowledge of various qualities that come into play in various actions of the development of personality. However, it is to be noted that value-oriented educational pattern requires a great professional competency. Education, today, is passing through a phase of transition. From pre-independence to post-independence, it has come a long way. There is now a lot of knowledge explosion and the technical know-how has not only accelerated the process of growth but also entanced the possibilities of growth and betterment of life. It has therefore become necessary to work for spiritual, moral and social upliftment of entire human kind and make them know the importance of moral values. But for all this, to understand about the psychological parameters of value, it is a must.

Correct to state that values are acquired at a early stage from the environment also. To make the same formation of opinion for the behaviours related to a value code, depend only on situation in which an individual is working. It does not depend on his or her feelings but depend on environment too. So also, some value component may react directly to the same learner clientele under different learning opportunities and situations. The behaviour that is value-based help to solve his or her problems with the help of his or her potentialities. Achieving the appropriate results he or she gets satisfaciton and accept the related positive values. It is called assimilation. Now, he or she learns to select those values which are positive and appreciable. He or she rejects those negative values which are not appreciable and which do not give any satisfaction after using them. In fact, such values do not solve his or her problems because these are false. Hence, it is true to say that selection and rejection of value becomes possible by power of judgement and evaluation. The learner is thus able to compare the value and then find new avenues for exercising the positive values; and thereby he or she select or disseminate the particular type of values.

On the basis of the above said facts the school curricular activities should be constructed in such a way that they become helpful for exercising value. Side by side, the pupil should be made quite sensitive, courageous and honest to accept and exercise the positive values. Further, it must be added that the pupil must also be mad aware about sharing the values. In fact, exercising of values takes place through interaction, imagination and symbolising judgement, decision, and potentialities are the pre-requisities of value inculcation.

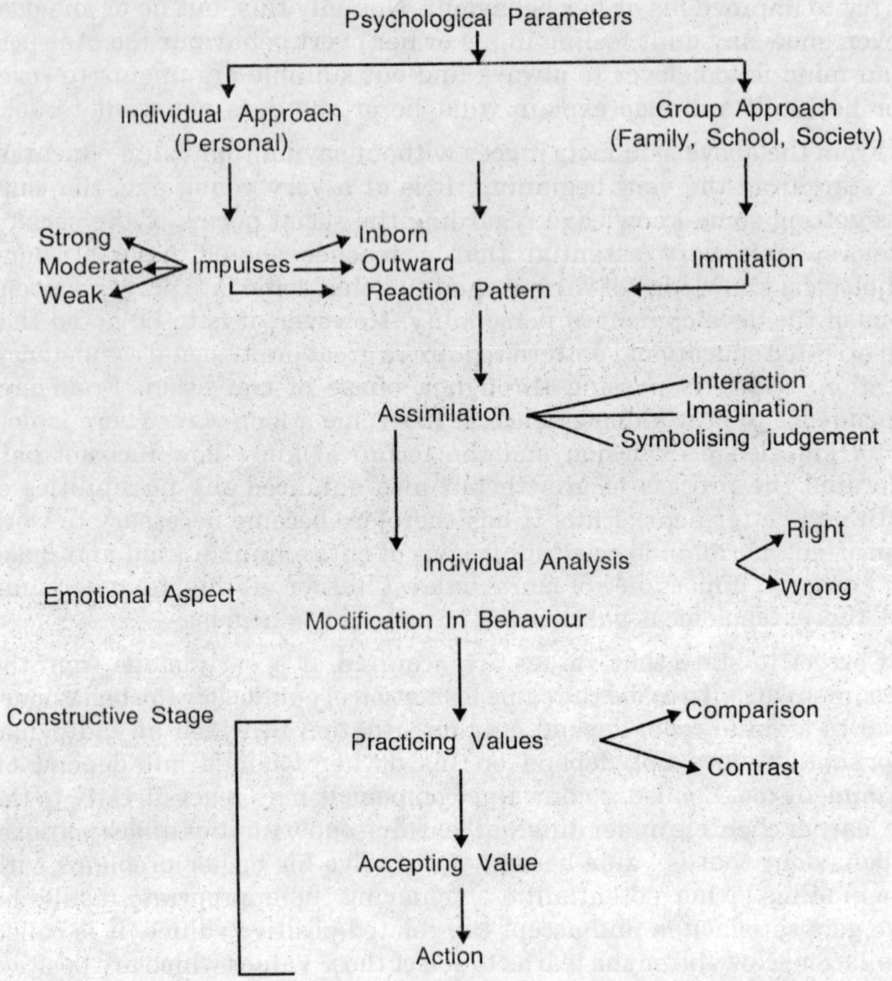

Acquisition of knowledge and system of representation of value are two important aspects of learning values. Acquisition depends on the intelligence of the pupil which help him or her internalisation of the values; and for lisation, interaction is required.

Confidence is needed for exercising the values. It is that component by which the pupil can use his or her potential fully. But, if the pupil is not confident and does not utilise his or her potentialities while exercising a particular value, he or she will not get success in the task undertaken. This leads to a week desire to accept positive values and there are all likely chances that the pupil might get into frustration or anxiety. It may also happen that if situation becomes worse due to frustration, he or she might embrace self-annihilation because of failures. However, instead of evaluating causes of failures and rectifying the errors, pupil accepts failure as a negative value.

EDUCATION IN VALUES AND SPIRITUALITY

15

Excessive consumerism, knowledge bang, value crisis, cultural lag, commecialisation of services, extremism, terrorism, communalism and many more evils are disturbing our social systems. The greatest challenge before us today is: how to be a true human under modern conditions. In this era of unprecedented social upsurge, teachers' education should have greater and more scarifying involvements in negotiating the biased and sentimental views of life amid the teaching and the pupil community. Value crisis in education and the need for fresh recharge of the entire system for a new lease of life with direly needed values seems to be the common cry of teachers, educationists, academicians, administrators and generally all those who have some conscience and have spent some time reflecting on the spiralling downfall of human values in National life. The growing fear of the serious lacuna in terms of values in all educational programmes are being increasingly lamented over, more so that the said lacuna that had indented itself into national life in the past few decades is being brutally dimensionalised into communal riots and frenzy, religious hatred and violence, horrific killings and bloodshed and powerful lease of terror even in the campus of educational institutions. It is fully apparent that education today has become a mechanical, information giving and examination oriented activity weaning the learners away from societal needs and realities as well as the niceties and refinements of personality, behaviour and character. A considerable decline is discernable in moral, social, cultural and national ethos which have left ugly and unpleasant impressions on the Indian facade and resulted on a crisis of character and ethics at all levels of public and private life. Education is basically a process of nurturing, developing and shaping the thought process of children. Apart from its conventional information giving and skill developing role, its highest and noblest function is to help individuals become better human beings. Then only will education attain its true dimension of "Education for knowing, Education for doing and Education for becoming". The solution to our problem lies on the minds and hearts of the teacher in whose influential and powerful hands the civilised society has entrusted its precious human resources.

Values are set of principles. They influence our thoughts, feelings, action and guide us to do the right things. In this age of rapid social change influenced by technology there appears a value crisis in the society. The youth of today is living in more complex society. On the one hand they have experienced man on the moon and on the other hand they have witnessed social riots, war, poverty and corruption. To them the instructions are no longer temples of wisdom. They are someting like many marketplaces where there is no devotion nor respect and ultimately there has been increased sensitivity to the failure of our educational system to live upto the idealistic hopes. "The destiny of India is now being shaped in her classrooms". This statement is found in education commission report (1996). Character building as an object was stressed in curriculum framed by NCERT. Teacher must play an important role in inculcating values among students. They should develop nationalistic feelings; create awareness about the problems related to food, water, energy environment, pollution, health and population and give equal importance to all students irrespective of caste, sex and money.

There should be school programmes for developing values like community prayer, health and cleanliness programmes, citizenship training programmes, social service programmes celebration of national festivals. Education without vision is waste. Value based education is an unavoidable necessity.

Erosion of values in present day society is a matter of great concern for educationists and leaders from all over the world.

Modernisation and economic competition in the world market and a high degree of scientific and technological knowledge have provided comforts and fulfilled many needs. The emphasis today is on material development, production of a large variety of consumer goods and on raising economic standards. This has led to greater attention on education in technical subjects that provide immediate access to the job market.

Scientific and technical study may increase a student's knowledge of formulae and sharpen his memory and numerical faculties. However, without learning to apply the powers of reasoning and analysis to subjects like language, literature, social science, philosophy, history and political science, students are inadequately prepared for the breadth and depth of human life. There is a real danger of preoccupation with consumerism, and of finer feelings being overtaken by greed.

Today education in human and moral values has been disregarded and largely considered irrelevant as a preparation for life. Countries may produce well-trained scientits, engineers, doctors, lawyers, administrators, business executives, artists etc., however, society shows increasing signs of suffering from the consequent loss of human touch which have been displaced by materialism.

It is a matter of great concern that corruption, bribery and nepotism at various levels in the world are prevalent despite laws against them. Corruption means to use or be willing to use political or social power to perform dishonest or illegal actions in return for money or some advantage. The root of this attitude is greed.

Entire universe is suffering from an acute crisis of diminishing values. This is a very dangerous situation. To overcome this ethical crisis, it is necessary to educate the present generation in spiritual values, and this will be a correct approach to globalisation. It will automatically enrich the person's personality.

Education in values can make a significant impact on many of social ills that exist due to lack of values. At present, most people assume that corruption, bribery and nepotism are part of life. Education in values, through many channels of communication, will increase awareness and provide people of all ages as well as social groups with the necessary tools and skills to resist pressure to conform to such practices.

When education in values and spirtuality is integrated into technical education programmes and provided to both genders equally, it results in more balanced individuals who are properly equipped for civil life. Education in human values and spirituality contributes to shifting deeply entrenched social attitudes, which are antagonistic to women and people of lower caste who legally have the same rights as everyone else. Education in values also boosts the confidence of socially disadvantaged individuals and inspires them to claim their rights.

People in general will also be sensitised to the value of nature and the necessity of taking people care of natural environment. The dangers of environmental pollution and the irreversible damages caused by indiscriminate destruction of trees and animals are already well known. Education in values can inspire people to act upon that awareness. This form of education also serves to empower people to resist their tendencies to greed, selfishness and violence in thought, world and deed.

Through education in values and spirituality the public will be adequately informed about the dangers of drug use, gambling and other forms of addiction. They will also be taught skills to resist peer pressure. Education in values and spirituality has the scope for creating a world of people who are informed, sensitive and embodiments of the ideals of a society based in human, moral and spiritual values.

Attempts have been made to bring about social change through legislation and development programmes, however they have not been very successful, so educationists and researchers in social development are now saying that change is successful only when done at the individual level. A story that illustrates the power of the individual as an agent for change follows:

Once the father of young boy was very busy in his work. The boy came and interrupted him again and again. The father thought of a plan. He had before him a map of the world. He tore it up and asked the boy to put the pieces of the map back together. He thought it would take his son a lot of time, but the boy accomplished the task within two minutes. Greatly surprised, the father asked him how he was able to do it so quickly. The son's reply was, "It was so simple, Dad. There was the picture of a man on the other side of the paper. I just completed the picture of the man and the picture of the world was completed automatically.'

Education in values of the individual level demonstrates the power of an individual to influence society through example. People tend to act in an elevated way when present with an example of high standards. Examples are a powerful inspiration and motivator. People copy what they see for more readily than they obey spoken or written prescriptions. The words of guru or teacher are transformative only insofar as he or she is a living example. The saying goes: "Actions speak louder than words."

It is strongly felt that education in values and spirituality at the level of the individual enriches a person's personality. Voluntary simplicity of lifestyle saves a lot of expenditure, and protects a person from the temptation to add to his or her resources through unfair or dishonest means. An honest person is the same internally and externally. Without self-deception there are no double standards, no conflicts in the mind, and one is liked by others.

UNESCO (United Nations Education, Social and Cultural Organisation) has set up an International Commission under the chairmanship of Jacques Delors. It includes educators from around the world. The Delors Report identifies four pillars of education: Learning to know, Learning to do, Learning to be and Learning to live together. The first requires intellectual ability; the second requires acquisition of skills; the third and the fourth require inculcation of values.

Every society decides its own values and strives for the same through all its activities. Values referred to objects that human beings consider desirable and worthy of pursuit in their thoughts, feelings and actions. These may be material objects, such as food and clothes or abstract qualities like truth and honesty. Education is a deliberated effort of society to bring about desirable changes in the learners. Transmission of culture, values and ethics is a prime concern of education. But this task can't be performed in isolation, without keeping the social trends in view. If we examine the society around, it seems to be a wealth centred society, seeking comforts, pleasure and security through money only. Such society is hardly concerned for social harmony, personality, philosophy, principles, values and care for social well-being. A teacher has to understand this condition and along-with his regular task of imparting knowledge and skills, correct the mind set and view point of the society. Yet, the question “where have the values gone?” still remains answered.

CONCLUDING REMARKS

We are living in a globalised society today. The word ‘Gloabalisation’ is commonly used to describe the spread and connectedness of production, communication, knowledge, technologies and services across the world. This spread involves all aspects of social, economical and political life and even the values, ethics, traditions, lifestyle and thinking patterns. Education being a dynamic and deep impacting ingredient of social life is not an exception and is proceeding towards a new horizon through globalisation. Students are exposed to excessive knowledge today without discrimination for good and bad. As teachers, we are supposed to support the act of gaining knowledge from all possible corners and sources and keep the students concerned and concentrated to their prime concern of gaining knowledge for positive self-development.

RELEVANT SUGGESTIONS FOR IMPLEMENTING VALUE ORIENTATION IN TEACHER-EDUCATION

16

INTRODUCTION

Our society is culturally plural society; therefore, education should foster universal and eternal values oriented towards the unity and integration of our people. Such value-education should help eliminate religious fanaticism, violence and superstition. Over and above, one must note that value-education has a profound positive content which is based on our heritage, national goals and universal perceptions.

On the basis of the above said aspect, it is very much felt to suggest the objectives of Teacher-Education.

SUGGESTIONS FOR FRAMING OBJECTIVES OF TEACHER-EDUCATION

Having gone through the previous chapters, any lay-man may automatically come to the conclusion that the teacher is the main inspiring person behind the principles of value-education. Because, it is a teacher alone who can become the guiding light to drive away ignorance and also the care-taker of the future generation. Hence, the teacher's responsibility is to get high values not only in his or her personal life but also in the profession chosen. Now all such discussion means that the teacher must be well-trained before joining the chosen profession. It is here we come, to the understanding of a high place of teachers training institution. It is the teacher-educators who must themselves play a role of a care-taker in moulding their trainees. Accordingly, the objectives of teacher-education have been set which are as stated below:

Teacher-education institutions:

1. Must try to develop Gandhian values.
2. Must try to act as liaison between school and community.
3. Must try to perceive the role as that of a guide to the community.
4. Must try to have positive attitude towards the trainees in developing in them academic skills.
5. Must try to understand the socio-emotional personal problems of the trainees.
6. Must try to employ means for integrating community life with educational programmes.
7. Must try to help their trainees understand the objectives of school-education.
8. Must try to help their trainees understand the principles of teaching and learning.
9. Must try to foster all-round growth in their trainees, so that their trainees, in future, will be able to develop all-round growth of their students in their respective schools.
10. The teachers' training institutions must keep themselves busy with Action Research and investigatory projects thus, the climate of creativity should be rigorously promoted.
11. There should be orientation courses for the teacher-educators (with less experience) for three to four days in the beginning of every session to focus their attention on the needs, goals and means of value-orientation of teacher-educators curriculum.

Barring aside the above said objectives of teachers' training institutions, it is also essential to note the objectives of teaching values in teachers training colleges. Hence,

CERTAIN SUGGESTIONS REGARDING OBJECTIVES OF TEACHING VALUES IN TEACHERS' TRAINING COLLEGES:

A Pupil-Teacher or a trainee must be made clear of his or her learning of values while undergoing the training. Hence, it is necessary to know the objective of the same which have been suggested as follows:

The teachers training colleges should help the teacher-trainee —

1. In understanding the necessity of inculcating values in schools (primary as well as secondary)
2. In realising their roles as spiritual guides in schools
3. In picking up those aspects of the syllabus in their disciplines which may lead themselves for value-instructions
4. In involving effectively there would be pupils in learning the appropriate values through curricular and extra-curricular activities

5. In organising different types of activities there would be pupil's involvement in learning the concept of value-education.

SUGGESTED VALUE-EDUCATION PAPER IN TEACHER-EDUCATION

In the light of the facts discussed so far in all the previous chapters, the need arises for a well-defined programme of adaptation in Colleges of Education. Mere appending of a unit of value-education to the existing papers would not do justice to this important subject. Hence, a paper on VALUE-EDUCATION should be introduced in the B.Ed. Course. Regarding this, the following are the suggestions.

VALUE-EDUCATION PAPER: OBJECTIVES

The teacher trainees will

1. Understand the importance of values in human life and the necessity of value education.
2. Appreciate the basic principles of major religions of the world.
3. Acquire the knowledge of the greatness of Indian culture and the significance of our national goals.
4. Understand the relevance of the values advocated by great leaders.
5. Acquire the knowledge of value enshrined in Indian Constitution.
6. Understand the methods of inculcating values and the role of family, school and society.

SYLLABUS

UNIT - I

Values — Definition — Classification of values — Value consciousness — Importance of Values.

UNIT - II

Values emphasized in the scriptures of Major Religions of the World: Vedas and Upanishads, The Bhagawad Gita, The Quran and The Bible (Religious tolerance).

UNIT - III

Values advocated by Swami Vivekananda, Sri Ramakrishna Paramahamsa, Sri Sarada Devi, The Gandhian Values — Implications for education.

UNIT - IV

India's common cultural heritage and ethos — Values enshrined in Indian Constitution — Removal of social barriers — Equality of the gender — Inculcation of scientific temper — Small family norm — Protection of the environment.

UNIT - V

Importance of Peace and Co-operation — National Integration and International Understanding — Universal Brotherhood.

UNIT - VI

Traditional and modern values — Absolute and Relative values — Value Conflict — Value Crisis — Need for Value Education — Science and spirituality.

UNIT - VII

Levels of development of the Affective Domain — Internalisation of Values — Kohlberg's stages of Moral development.

UNIT - VIII

Inculcation of values — Curriculum of the school — School practices and traditions — Impact of the teachers — peer group.

UNIT - IX

Methods of teaching values — Direct and Indirect — Social Learning Model — Jurisprudential Inquiry — Model-Critical Incident Approach and Integrated Atmospherical Approach — Value Clarification Approach.

UNIT- X

Assessment of values — Observation, Cumulative Record, Anecdotal Record, Situational Tests — Value Scales, Projective Techniques.

UNIT - XI

Analysis of text book of Secondary classes — treatment of values.

PRACTICAL ASPECT OF VALUE EDUCATION IN COLLEGES OF EDUCATION

1. Morning assembly — prayers from different faiths — silent prayer - sayings of great persons — short speech by students on the life of great leaders, humanitarian, inventors — mass physical exercise.
2. Manual labour — social service — youth for mass literacy.
3. Observation of days of importance — participation in cultural activities.

4. Review of articles in magazines, programmes on radio, TV, films for depiction of values.
5. Preparation of album, conducting an exhibition on value theme.

DIRECTIONS TO TEACHERS (CLASSES V TO VII)

Some practical hints that result from the application of methods of psychological and value-oriented development are suggested here:

(*a*) It may be noted that a good many children are under the influence of the inner psychic presence which shows itself very distinctly at times in their spontaneous reactions and even in their words. All spontaneous turning to love, truth, beauty, knowledge, mobility, heroism is a sure sign of the psychic influence.

(b) To recognise these reactions and to encourage them wisely and with a psychic feeling would be the first indispensable step.

(*c*) The best qualities to develop in children are:

Sincerity
Honesty
Straightforwardness
Cheerfulness
Courage
Disinterestedness
Patience
Endurance
Perseverance
Peace
Calm
Self-control
Self-mastery
Truth
Harmony
Liberty

(*d*) These qualities are taught infinitely better and also by telling stories than by beautiful speeches.

(*e*) The undesirable impulses and habits should not be treated harshly. The child should not be scolded. Particularly, care should be taken not to rebuke a child for a fault which one commits oneself. Children are very keen and clear-sighted observers; they soon find out the educator's weaknesses and note them without pity.

(*f*) When a child makes a mistake, one must see that he confesses it to the teacher or the guardian spontaneously and frankly; and when he has confessed it, he should be made to understand with kindness and affection what was wrong in the movement and that he should not repeat it. A fault confessed must be forgiven.

(*g*) The child should be encouraged to think of wrong impulses not as sins or offences but as symptoms of a curable disease alterable by a steady and a sustained effort of the will — falsehood being rejected and replaced by truth, fear by courage, selfishness by sacrifice, malice by love.

(*h*) Great care should be taken to see that unformed virtues are not rejected as faults. The wildness and recklessness of many young natures are only the overflowing of an excessive strength, greatness and nobility.

(*i*) An affection that is firm yet gentle, sees clearly, and a sufficiently practical knowledge will create bonds of trust that are indispensable for the educator to make the education of a child effective.

(*j*) When a child asks a question, he should not be answered by saying that it is stupid or foolish, or that the answer will not be understood by him. Curiosity cannot be postponed, and an effort must be made to answer questions truthfully and in such a way as to make the answer comprehensible to his mental capacity.

(*k*) The teacher should ensure that the child gradually begins to be aware of the psychological centre of his being, the psychic being, the inner seat of the highest truth of our existence.

(*l*) With that growing awareness, the child should be taught to concentrate on this presence and make it more and more a living fact.

(*m*). The child should be taught that whenever there is an inner uneasiness, he should not pass it off and try to forget it, but should attend to it, and try to find out by an inner observation the cause of the uneasiness, so that it can be removed by inner or other methods.

(*n*) It should be emphasized that if one has a sincere and steady aspiration, a persistent and dynamic will, one is sure to meet in one way or another, externally by study and instruction, internally by concentration, revelation or experience, the help one needs to reach the goal. Only one thing is absolutely indispensable, the will to discover and realise. This discovery and this realisation should be the primary occupation of the being, the pearl of great price which one should acquire at any cost. Whatever one does, whatever one's occupation and activity, the will to find the truth of one's being and to unite with it must always be living, always present behind all one does, all that one thinks, all that one experiences.

All the above suggestions are to be implemented from day-to-day under various circumstances and in the context of living problems of the growth of children.

The role of the teacher is to put the child upon the right road to his own perfection and encourage him to follow it, watching, suggesting, helping, but not imposing or interfering. The best method of suggestion is by personal example, daily conversation and books read from day-to-day.

GENERAL SUGGESTIONS

1. A good source book or learning package should be developed on the theme "VALUE FOR TEACHERS OF THE EMERGING INDIAN SOCIETY".
2. The orientation courses and refresher courses conducted by the Academic Staff Colleges should mould their programmes to offer the teacher-educators a sound basis in value-education.
3. Special care has to be taken while framing the curriculum, to ensure that the theme of value-education receives utmost importance. There is great need to develop new, teaching and learning materials in relation to value-education.
4. Special programmes on TV should be telecast which will bring to the pupils the inspiring message of value-education.
5. Art exhibitions, musical performances may also be organised on values concerned with national integration, secularism, dignity of labour.
6. Intra as well as inter school competitions should be held in music, literature, dance, drama, sports and games. At present it is felt essential as well as imperative on the part of the school to provide pupils with all kinds of facilities for gaining learning experiences not only in intellectual and physical areas, but also in the moral, social, emotional and aesthetic aspects so that the citizens of tomorrow develop all-round personalities.
7. Drama, Folk-Dances, Folk-Music, Abhangas Recitations relating to the unity of our heritage, Patriotic Anecdotes, etc. may be occasionally arranged to promote desired values among the pupils.
8. With a view to making education an effective medium for cultivation of values, value-education should be imparted with teaching basic values to pupils through interesting discussions and practical applications. True value-education consists in the teacher's conscientious endeavour to enable their pupils to discover themselves and their reliable possibilities. But what is happening today? Nothing but spoon-feeding, "Both teachers as well as

students are rather like a reluctant team of bullocks yoked together to draw water from a well that has run dry!" says K. G. Saiyidian, and it is really true.

9. The school Annual-Day Prize Distribution Ceremony, School Festivals like Ganesh and Saraswathi Poojas, National Festivals like Independenc Day, Republic Day, should be celebrated involving pupils to a greater extent. Variety entertainment programmes, drama, one-act plays, a national theme or historical episode may be enacted on occasions.
10. There is no denying of the fact that value-development is an important part of school curriculum. But the question is "What values are to be taught in schools?" We have already discussed that values are various types such as relating to personal and social living, spiritual and religious aspects, economic and monetary values and multitude of other belonging to the educational experience of the children. It is a controversial matter which spiritual values are to be taught in the school or is it purely the function of religious institutions whatever may be the approach. What we should do is to give top priority to personal and social values as compared to other values, as it is a function of education to make the students as good citizens of the society. Social concepts that involve value-oriented behaviour must be discussed in the classroom.
11. Another group of concepts that cause trouble for the young students involve their relationships with our society. Laws are passed and enforced for the protection of individuals which have a rightful place in any system of values. Yet, our youths challenge society's rights to regular affairs that involve their personal desires. They should be taught to respect these laws and if they want to change them, they should do it through the democractic process.
12. For successful social living, children should be taught that traditional social institutions such as family, school have a valuable place in our culture. Without the school, social and persoanl progress would be severely handicapped and children must be made aware of the tremendous influence of education upon their present and future lives.
13. Values that relate to the prerservation of human life certainly belong to the educative process. All children should be made aware of the value of human life and also of changes of impulsive action, carelessness, thrill-seeking and other actions that destroy lives. They should also be taught the value of enjoying the accomplishment of work and have pride in self-sufficiency.

14. Another technique helpful in the teaching of values is a discussion that involves the study of ideas and ideals presented intellectually as a part of organised subject matter of the curriculum. A study of the philosophical view points makes the students aware of the values that should be developed. Moreover, the teacher should also point out the values as they are shown in movies. Art creations and moral or social situations that become a part of classroom activity. The school offers many opportunities for transmitting similar positive values. For many boys and girls the school is the only setting in which they are exposed to the culture's best literature, art and music. If these experiences can be made a pleasurable of the school's curricular and extra-curricular offerings, there is a good chance that pupils will adopt them as positive values.

15. The teacher can do many things to influence the values of his students. Probably his best approach is the indirect one, of exhibiting sympathy and understanding towards his pupils. If he is successful in projecting a genuine concern for each pupil's happiness and welfare, he will exert strong influence on his values. He can, through personal suggestions and group discussion, have a significant influence. He can also take the aid of radio, television, movies, books, newspapers, etc. to provide valuable opportunities for pupils to explore their own value system.

16. There are some models of teaching which can be utilised in the area of value-education. One such model in the Jurisprudential Inquiry Model of Teaching which help students to develop the capacity for analysing social issues to assume the role of others and social dialogue.

The Jurisprudential Inquiry Model is one of the value-clarification techniques. The process of value-clarification in the Jurisprudential Inquiry Model beings with the presentation of a case involving a dilemma, cases pertaining to legalising mercy killing, legalising abortion, death sentence, etc. are selected. In the presentation of the case, facts are reviewed viz., should mercy killing be legalised? Or should the government decide about the life and death of an ailing citizen? One may come up with several policy, issue e.g., one may say that mercy killing should be legalised. What values are upheld by the person who puts their statement? Is it saving resources of the country or is it humanness that is concern or compassion for the suffering? Thus, some may feel that mercy killing should be legalised while others may feel the contrary. Once the teacher-educators are fully equipped with the Jurisprudential Inquiry Model, the knowledge will be automatically transferred to the trainees. Such a trained teacher will be able to handle efficiently the subject of value-education in schools. Then, it can also be useful for the teacher in making the pupils understand (particularly of Std. IX and X) and develop their ability to analyse public issues and clarify value positions. Such sort of discussions will also prove to be useful for the teachers in:

1. Helping the students prove the desirable and undesirable consequences of their stand.
2. Helping their students to use analogies.
3. Helping their students in setting priorities of one value over the other.

VALUE EDUCATION INITIATIVES: A FUTURE VISION

17

INTRODUCTION

These has been much to feel elated in the current terms. The knowledge 'explosion' has extended the mental horizons of human beings. Utilisation of skill and knowledge has brought economic affluence and political power to some. There are also areas of serious concern which have emerged prominently. The domain of human values continues to erode. The crisis of human values is worsening and its shadow looms large. The calm and peace which could be an outcome of advancing knowledge and technological development is being shattered by turbulence, disturbance, conflict and distrust everywhere. It is not that mankind lacks knowledge and skills, but it is wisdom, character and values which are in crisis. The economic and technological values are in conflict with 'human values.' In a world which is primarily torn between a few 'haves' and majority of 'have nots' in a highly disproportionate manner, tensions, diversities, violence, terrorism, consumerism and the like are creating a dreadful scenario. Education can be the universal hope. Education can contribute immensely to the culture of peace, social cohesion and international collaboration. Crisis of values needs to be seen both at individual and societal level. In individual it manifests itself in a sense of drift and helplessness, in an alienation of meaning and purpose of life and living. The alienation may be the rersult of neglect, poverty and impact of technological presence. The individual has become an object of manipulated disposition. At the societal level the crisis is manifested by increasing fragmentation and divisions of population, in the diminution of human relationship, increasing exploitation and consequent degradation of the natural environment, diminishing concern for the future and increase in all forms of violence.

Education is the most powerful instrument for achieving social cohesion and harmony. In Indian context the national goals include internalising secularism, strengthening democracy, ensuring equality, striving for national integration, revamping fraternity, providing social justice and liberty. The system of education must perceive human needs, perceptions and aspirations. It must develop respect for awareness of human rights. It is essential that every child internalise the fundamental duties as enlisted in Article 51 (A) of the Constitution. Unity and integrity of India, harmony, spirit of common brotherhood, preservation of rich cultural heritage of our composite culture, compassion, scientific temper, humanism, adjuring violence, etc. have been included in fundamental duties incorporated in Indian Constitution by 42nd Amendment. These also highlight the need to improve the protect natural environment, develop scientific temper, humanism and spirit of enquiry. No education system can ignore these aspects. Every child needs to internalise the values enshrined in our constitution, the values that have developed in cultural contexts and could be derived from our heritage. The Delor's Common Report, (UNESCO, 1996) very strongly recommended to every country that their education system should be 'rooted to culture and committed to progrss.' The Commission visualised social cohesion and 'Learning to live together' as most important objectives of education of 21st century. Education for peace and for a culture of peace is being globally accepted and adopted by the nations and more so by the education systems worldwide. In India, the social cohesion, adherence to moral and ethical values and commitment to the society have been the hallmarks of socio-cultural ethos. Gandhiji had identified truth and non-violence as the two central pillars to ensure peace, prosperity, progress and perfection in thought and deed of every individual. In Upanishada, the guru advises his disciple who desires peace of mind to persue three-fold paths of (*a*) knowledge to end conflict with nature (*b*) service to end the internal conflict of mind when many pleasures are greedily sought from life. Threat posed by LPG (Liberalisation, Privatisation and Globalisation) in the shape of cut-throat competition, materialism, decline of values, rise of consumerism and technological culture to the acculturating role of education, traditional values and objectives of education as perceived by great Indian thinkers, philosophers and educators needs to be analysed carefully. There is a great danger that the acculturating role of education may be relegated to the background and the influence of market forces and materialistic pursuits may overrun the traditional values. Promotion of value oriented education thus becomes one of the critical ingredient of educational process. NCERT has a role to play. It has responded by adopting multiple strategies to strengthen value-orientation and value inculcation at all levels of school education in the country.

NCERT'S MANDATE

The mandate of NCERT is to advise and assist the Government of India in formulation and implementation of policies and major programmes in the field of school education and also to assist and collaborate with state education departments in the implementation of their policies and programmes in the area of school education. During the last forty years NCERT and its constituent units have assisted in promoting quality and standard of school education, helped in building capacity of state-level resource institutions and developed partnership and linkages with state departments of education and state level resource institutions through inputs line development of curriculum and instructional materials, training, research, survey, extension activities, innovation, experimentation, documentation and dissemination. Education is in the concurrent list of the Constitution of India. NCERT is not a statutory but an advisory body. State Governments develop their own syllabi, text book and other materials through their own agencies. NCERT assists in such initiatives. Its professional credibility has been well established and it has also been appreciated by state agencies and institutions.

VALUE EDUCATION INITIATIVES

Educational Initiatives of the post-independence period have unequivocally included emphasis on value in education. These are prominently included in recommendations of Kothari Commission (1964-66), curriculum for the ten-year school: A Framework (1975), National Policy of Education (1986 with 1992 modifications), National Curriculum Framework (1988) and the recommendations of Parliamentary Standing Committee on Human Resource Development — Eighty First Report on Value based Education (1999). National Curriculum Framework for school education (2000) has observed that 'Truth, righteous conduct, peace, love and non-violence are the core universal values that can become the foundation for building the value based education programme .... These five universal values represent the five domains of human personality intellectual, physical, emotional, psychological and spiritual — are correlated with the five major objectives of education, namely knowledge, skill, balance, vision and identity." In addition, key qualities like regularity, punctuality, cleanliness, self-control, industriousness, sense of duty, desire to serve, responsibility, enterprise, sensitivity to equality, fraternity, democractic attitude and sense of obligation to environmental protection have been highlighted. The framework has proposed inculcation and nurturance of moral, ethical, humanistic and constitutional values.

> Violence is the weapon of the weak;
> Non-violence; that of the strong
>
> He who has neither peace nor strength
> Of mind, how can he have knowledge?
>
> Pure love removes all weariness
>
> Without truth it is impossible to observe
> any principles or rules in life.
> There must be truth in thought
> Truth in speech and Truth in action
>
> — *Mahatma Gandhi*

The Kothari Commission (1964-66) had observed that 'A new pride and a deeper faith expressed in living for the noble ideals of peace and freedom, truth and compassion are now needed.' As early as 1966, the Commission made significant recommendations about "Education on Social, Moral and Spiritual Values" in chapter VII on 'School Curriculum' and use of direct and indirect method in teaching of human values, which are still relevant.

- A man's value does not depend on what he learn or his position or fame, or what he does, but on what he is and inwardly becomes.
- Truth is the foundation of real spirituality and courage is its soul.
- Love leads us from suffering of division into the bliss of perfect union.

— *Sri Aurobindo*

National Curriculum Framework (2000) has recommended education about religion and not religious values. Awareness of religions has been conceived as one of the major source of values. The Framework observed that "What is required today is not religious education but education about religion, their basics, the values inherent therein and also a comparative study of the Philosophy of all religions. These needs to be inculcated at appropriate stages of education right from primary years. Students have to be given awareness that the essence of every religion is common, only the practices differ". The students should also be led to believe that differences of opinion in certain areas are also to be respected (p. 19). The framework had added caution that:

'Education about religion must be handled with great care. All steps must be taken advance to ensure that no personal prejudice or narrow minded perception are allowed to distort the real purpose of this venture and no rituals, dogmas and superstitions are propagated in the name of education about religion. All religions therefore are to be treated with equal respect (Sarva Dharma Sambhav) and there has to be no discrimination on the ground of any religion (Pathanirapekstata) (p. 20).

The Parliamentary Standing Committee on Human Resource Development – Eighty First Report on Value based Education (1999) (Chavan Committee's Report) submitted in both houses of Parliament observed that Truth (Satya), Righteous conduct (Dharma), peace (Shanti), Love (Prema) and Non-violence (Ahimsa) are the Core Universal Values which can be identified as the foundation stone on which the value based education programmes can be built up'.

The report of the Committee in para 13 has also made significant observations:

'Another aspect that must be given some thought is religion, which is most misused and misunderstood concept. The process of making the students acquainted with the basis of all religions, the values inherent therein and also a comparative study of the philosophy of all religions should begin at the middle stage in schools and continue upto the university level. The students have to be made aware that the concept behind every religion is common, only the practices differ. Even if there are differences of opinion to certain areas people have to learn to co-exist and carry no hatred against any religion'.

The ideas as elaborated are essentially based on the recommendations of the Kothari Commission 1964-66, National Policy of Education 1986 and the S. B. Chavan Committee's Report, 1999. The Kothari Commission has observed that:

'In such a society, however, one had to make a distinction between 'religious education' and 'education about religions'. The former is largely concerned with the teaching of the tenets and practices of a particular religion, generally in the form in which the religious group envisages them, whereas the latter is a study of religions and religons thought form a broad point of view — the internal quest of the spirit'. (Page 20, para 1.79).

The Commission had commended that:

"It is, however, necessary for a multi-relgious democratic state to promote a tolerant study of all religions so that its citizens can understand each other better and live amicably together .... we suggest that a syllabus giving well-chosen information about each of the major religion should be included as a part of the course in citizenship or as part of general education to be introduced in schools and colleges upto the first degree". (p. 20-21, para 1.79).

The Curriculum for Ten-Year School — A Framework (1975) had emphasised the need of character building and cultivation of human values.

National Curriculum Framework (1986) had highlighted the need of character building and inculcation of social and moral values (p. 5) and values for strengthening of national identity and unity (p. 5) and prerservation of cultural heritage and traditions (p. 4).

> Through law we find the freedom of peace in the external world of existence, through Goodness or Love we find our freedom in the world of deeper social relationship. Such freedom of realisation is possible only because supreme Truth is Shantam, is Shivam, is Peace, is Goodness, is Love".
>
> — *Rabindranath Tagore*

National Policy on Education 1986, in part VIII para 8.5 had made the following observations:

- 'In our culturally plural society, education should foster eternal values, oriented towards the unity and integration of our people'.
- '...............Value education has a profound positive content, based on our heritage, national goals, universal perceptions.'

In part XII under the heading "The future" NPE (1986) had further observed that.

- This future shape of education in India is too complex to envision with precision. Yet, given our tradition which always put a high premium on intellectual and spiritual attainment we are bound to succeed in achieving our objective.
- The Programme of Action and National Policy on Education 1986 in the chapter entitled 'The Cultural Perspective' under sub-heading 'Institutes of Moral Education' at the end assigned the task NCERT:

'A special place has been assigned to imparting of value oriented education in the Education Policy document. A beginning would be made by instituting a special study on value oriented education. Based on its analysis, it would in collaboration with NCERT and state institutions, help in suggestion broad parameters of values of integrity, truth, devotion, loyalty etc. with particular reference to their embodiment in Indian heritage, so as to blend naturally with the overall educational process" (p. 176).

APPROACH OF VALUE EDUCATION

The NCERT approach to value education has been summarised as follows:

- The Curriculum Framework for School Education has observed that: value education and education about religious would not form a separate subject of study for examination at any stage. These would be so judiciously integrated with all subjects of study in the scholastic areas that the objectives thereof would be directly and indirectly achieved in the classroom, at the school assembly places, play grounds, cultural centres and other rich places'.
- Every teacher has to be a teacher of values.
- Every activity, unit, textbooks and classroom interaction should be examined from the point of view of value identification/ inculcation and reinforcement and appropriate strategy needs to be evolved.
- Value education needs to be integrated to all activities of the school, classroom teaching, games, cultural activities, welfare services, help to needy students, remediation and narturing of talent, etc.

GENERAL INTERVENTIONS IN VALUE EDUCATION

The interventions in the teaching-learning process must:

- highlight the values inherent in different subject area.
- provide opportunities for questioning, sharing and practising values.

- provide opportunities for learning democratic principles.
- emphasize equalities of gender, social caste, classes and religion.
- underlines human rights, rights of the child, environmental protection, healthy living, etc.
- make the classroom atmosphere tension free and democratic to enhance values.
- encourage exhibitions, Bal-melas, Fairs and Folk cultural activities.
- provide appropriate guidance and counselling.
- organise inter-state cultural exchange programme.

STAGE SPECIFIC INPUTS

The exemplar activities at different stages are highlighted below:

At Elementary Stage

- the school assembly, group singing, practicing silence and meditation.
- simple and interesting stories about the lives and teaching of prophets, saints and sacred texts of different religions.
- field activities like game and sports, social work leading to the attitude of service (seva) to humanity and other creatures, and even to nature.
- cultural activities, plays etc. on appripriate theme.

At the Secondary/Higher Secondary Stages there should be arrangement of

1. morning assembly, reading from books of wisdom, great literature or an appropriate address by a teacher or a guest speaker.
2. essential teachings of major world religions, comparative study of the philosophy of religion.
3. social service during holidays outside school hours.
4. community singing programmes, National Integration Camps, the National Social Service, National Cadet Corps, Scouts and guides programme.
5. cultural activities, play, debates etc. on appropriate themes.

School may organise joint celebrations of the important occasions and festivals of major religious and cultural groups.

ROLE OF TEACHERS

The criticality of the role of teachers is well established and widely acknowledged. They have to be professionally prepared and made to internalise their role in value inculcation. Since every teacher is a value educator it is expected that he/she:

(i) Would develop a clear vision of their role in value orientation.

(ii) Would be able to identify the potential of different subjects and situations in school for fostering universal human values and be sensitized about their own influence as role models.

(iii) Would be able to analyse their own biases and attitude towards students.

(iv) Would evolve a positive approach to authentic orientation related to different religion and religion related values.

(v) Would be a good communicator.

(vi) Would be able to delineate stage specific strategies.

SUPPORTIVE INITIATIVES

A National Resource Centre for Value Education (NRCVE) has been set up at NCERT as an outcome of strategic planning to realise the objectives of value-based education at the school stage in the country. The Centre was inaugurated on 14th September, 2000. All the constituents of NCERT have been taking up programme in the area of value education under the aegies of NRCVE. The goals and functions of the centre are to:

- A reference library has been set up and is being enriched continuously. A wide variety of resource materials on value education like books, journals, other print materials, audio and video cassettes, CDs/multimedia packages, etc. are being continuously procured. The Centre has also procured literature on values enshrined in different religions and literature for children.
- Networking with organisation/NGOs working in the area of value education has been taken up with a view to develop linkages with various organisations/NGOs, within and outside India, working in the area of value education. Information about 300 organisations including their aims, nature of activities and publications have been procured and a directory of these organisations has already been brought out. The database could be accessed on the website of NCERT.
- The Journal of Value Education was launched under the aegies of National Resources Centre or Value Education, NCERT, in order to provide a forum for expression and sharing of issues related to education in human values among students and teachers at all levels, as well as the parents and the community.
- Identification and compilcation of materials/references of books, journals, articles, Ph.D. researches, NGOs' work and audio-video programmes brought out/published in English and Hindi in the country on value education in India are in progress in the seven constituent units of NCERT covering all the regions of the country.

- Recently on recommendations of NCERT Department of Education, MHRD has declared prominent NGOs like Ramakrishna Institute of Moral and Spiritual Education (RIMSE), Mysore, Sri Aurobindo Education Society, New Delhi, Chinmoy Mission, Prajapita Brahma Kumaris Iswariya Viswa Vidyalaya, Santi Kunj, Hardwar, Kendriya Jeevan Vigyan Academy, National Spiritual Assembly of Bahais of India and Sri Satya Sai Institute of Higher Learning as Regional Resource Centres on Value Education. NCERT is to coordinate and guide the activities of the Regional Resource Centres in the area of in-service education of teachers at all levels and for promotion of research related to value education. The NRCEV has also initiated:
  - development of a framework on value education in schools.
  - conceptualisation of some important values such as caring, excellence, creativity, spirituality, etc.
  - development of materials such as supplementary reading material for children, audio cassettes, video cassettes and multimedia.
  - development of training materials for teachers and teacher educators.
  - media mobilisation for awareness generation, training and preparation of resource materials, etc.
  - the revival of the community singing programme which is being organised by all constituent units in order to promote values among school children. Several state level organisations have shown keen interest in the programme.

TEACHER EDUCATION

Curriculum Framework for Quality Teacher Education of the statutory National Council for Teacher Education, (NCTE, 1998) has highlighted that the student-teachers should be capable of understanding the importance of value education, able to interpret values in the contemporary context and evolve strategies of imbibing these by students.

The concerns, issues related to strategies/approaches of value inculcation, integration of value activities with all programmes of the school and with the curriculum, textbooks, workbooks, multimedia and production of materials needs to be incorporated with pre-service teacher preparation of all levels of school education. Value education issues and methodology have been integrated in the innovative 2 years B.Ed. programme and 1 year Diploma course in Counselling and Guidance offfered by the Regional Institute of Education of NCERT. Similarly, the design of in-service education of the teachers, principals of schools and DIET faculty needs to be relooked at and the concern, issues, approaches related to value education will have to be incorporated therein. NCERT has incorporated value education related issues in the redesigned Special Orientation programmes for Primary Teachers (SOPT) and in the in-service training design for DIET faculty and DIET principles. In practically all the in-service training programmes organised by different constituent units of NCERT, the innovative methods/strategies of value education are being highlighted.

The teachers comprehension need not extend only to transmitting information from a prescribed textbook to the children but in developing capabilities to evolve the curriculum from the surroundings itself at the primary stage of school education. In developing such an approach, the critically of the need for value inculcation and emphasis on ethical and moral education should form an integral part of each and every unit and activity. Small stories and parables drawn from epics, mythologies and history suitable to the stage and linked to the value inculcation would generate interest amongst the young learners and could familiarise with the cultural evolution and heritage. This would also lead to understanding of the culture and heritage of different communities and gradually help in developing respect for religions, languages and cultural practices which may be different from that being practiced.

Teacher preparation must ensure development of commitment amongst teachers. It is a tough proposition when most of the other sectors are influenced by self-interest and material pursuits everywhere. However, teacher education needs to emphasise throughout each programme that teachers alone can kindle the spirit of value based growth and development and motivate other to lead their life with full commitment and adherence to common values as imbibed in the constitution of India.

MATERIAL DEVELOPMENT

- There is need to develop supplementary reading materials for school children based on stories and parables available/developed on value themes.
- Following example of NCERT, community singing programme needs to be extended to schools on a large scale and material prepared for the same in each language.
- Audio, video and multimedia modes need to be explored in a large scale for production of materials.

RESEARCH

Institutions working in the area have primarily been concerned with development and extension aspect of values and not much efforts have been made on research and innovation in the area. NCERT recently has already funded a number of research projects on value education.

— analysis of value education programme of an institution/ organisation through case study.

— experimental study to find out the effectiveness of different interventions applied for value inculcation in school system.

— development of instruments to measure value climate of schools.

— field testing of effective methods of value inculcation in schools.

— identification of effective methods for resolving value conflicts — conflict between societal value, vis-a-vis school value, conflict between school value vis-a-vis values propagated by media, etc.

— methodology of integration of values of text books and other instructional materials in different classes.

— integration of value related issues to teachers training programmes with focus on value integration to methodology of transaction.

— conduct of innovations/experimentations on value education.

— conceptual clarification, classification and behaviour specification of values.

— methodology of developing cooperation between home and school for value development.

— instructional strategies for trasaction of value related topics/ themes.

— identification of indigenous approach of value development for incorporation in pedagogy for schools.

— exploring mythologies of sustaining values among school children.

— exploring methologies of value inculcation through community involvement.

— identification of Sociological, psychological, cultural and technological factors influencing values.

— study on value preferences of different groups of school children.

— development and try out of an integrated approach a combination of methods approaches/programmes for promotion of values in schools.

TASKS AHEAD

There is a need to disseminate the messages related to value education in a mission mode to the schools located in district and sub-district level. The action plan of this respect will inclde:

- development of decentralised management structure with networking and linkages for implementing the programme on value education at state, district and grass root levels and its monitoring.

- development of strategies for massive awareness generation/ sensitisation programme on value education.
- development of strategies for material development relevant to school system and teacher education system using print, non-print including multimedia.
- strategies of integrating value education issues, mythologies and transactional approaches to the training programmes for teachers and teacher educators.
- to evolve minimum standard in education of human values and development of a framework of value-education.
- creation of a separate value education website for networking and dissemination.
- documentation and dissemination of strategies for nurturing universal human values.
- media mobilisation activities with specific focus on multimedia packages on value education and the use of information technology in sharing and dissemination of value education issues.

CONCLUSION

With all the limitations, deficiencies and rigidities inherent in our educational system and functioning of the schools and other learning centres, transformation overhauling of the system needs to be achieved only through the combined efforts of the teachers, institution/organisations and the communities. A value based approach must form the backbone of the educational system and also the teacher education system. Effective and visible steps needs to be formulated by the teacher education institutions and motivated schools at the earliest. It is hoped that the multiplier effects in this regard would be tremendous.

ROLE OF VALUES IN TEACHER-EMPOWERMENT

18

The quality of teaching irrespective of the resources available is determined by teacher quality; and excellence in any learning enterprise, is directly linked to the professional preparedness, dedication and willingness of the teachers. It is teacher who is responsible for providing an enabling environment for pupils to learn by enriching the national curricula using the appropriate textbooks and other resources. Teachers need to be able to transform their classrooms into dynamic pupil-centred learning environment. However, for all such said things, empowerment of the teacher is very much essential. Now, the question that jumps up is "WHAT IS TEACHER-EMPOWERMENT?" According to BOLIN, "Teacher-empowerment means investing teachers with the right to participate in the determination of school goals and policies and to exercise professional judgement about what and how to teach."

For teachers to be able to help the nation to realise the purpose for which the current massive educational reform has to take place, they need to be empowered. In fact, a teacher-empowerment is that process which makes school participants develope the competancy to take charge of their own professional growth and resolve their own problems. In the process, teachers are made to develop the belief that they have the required skills and knowledge to improve situations in which they operate. Issues that readily come to mind on teacher-empowerment include teacher participation in curriculum development, assessment participation, providing right training and retraining (in-service training), economic empowerment and conducive teaching environment (i.e., right equipment, adequate facilities, right leadership, etc.).

There are altogether six dimensions of teacher-empowerment; and these are —

Decision-making,

Professional growth,

Status,

Self-efficacy,

Autonomy, and

Impact.

Over and above, there seem to be four assumptions that regard teacher-empowerment. These are —

1. Teacher-empowerment is most effective when it is oriented to increase teacher professionalism.
2. Teacher empowerment has at least two dimensions : organisational and classroom.
3. Empowering teachers have the greatest impact on pupil achievement when the emphasis is on the core technology of teaching and learning in schools.
4. To be effective, teacher-empowerment needs to be authentic.

Teacher empowerment, thus, therefore, perceived as a crucial factor that affects school effectiveness. In fact, the term Teacher Empowerment is very ambiguous and it is really difficult to define. It is a relative teem and consists of two words — 'Teacher' and 'Empowerment'. 'Teacher' means a person who has teaching skills and possesses certain professional qualities of teaching. 'Empowerment' is a relative term and refers to some criteria. Empowerment is considered as development of skills to make a person more confident, self-reliant and develop ability to take self-decision.

The teacher is empowered to the extent that his or her path is favourable for his or her development of basic skills, understanding, work habits, desirable attitudes, value judgement and adequate personal adjustment of pupils. Apart from teaching and maintaining a relationship, an empowered teacher also includes in service work, attending conferences, professional reading and being a member a matter of professional organisation. An empowered teacher is time-conscious also. Being time-conscious means accomplishing all the duties and responsibilities on time, especially when it comes to submitting report grades, question papers, etc. Empowerment, thus, is that process whereby the teachers develop the competence to take charge of their own growth. Empowered individuals have the skills and knowledge and also values which help them to act on a situation and improve it. In fact, the values help the empowered teachers to gain the opportunity in decision-making. Knowledge must be seen as a means of teacher empowerment rather than of gaining power. Hammond (1997) has rightly put — "empowerment must occur through knowledge rather than through new controls that would enfrachise teacher at the cost of others, especially parents who have a deep interest in children's success."

Empowerment, thus means to give somebody the power to do something or to give more control over their work and; Teacher-empowerment means the empowerment of teachers. Teacher empowerment is very essential to achieve the goal of real education, to link education with life and to make education meaningful. Accordingly, the most important values for the teacher empowerment are —

regularity,
time-keeping,
humanity,
curiosity,
friendship,
responsibility,
clarity,
dutifulness,
patriotism,
kindness,
trust in truth and
national integration.

Empowerment enables the teacher to gain insight and have an awareness what is undeservable and unfavourable about his or her current situation. Empowerment transpires over time and usually it is not instantaneous. It means building aspirations, hopes and expectations. In a nutshell, it is the ability to direct and control one's own life. Hence, the importance of teacher-empowerment in key education areas cannot be underestimated. Empowering teachers has its greatest impact on pupil achievement when the emphasis is on the core values of teaching and learning in schools. In the present context, teacher empowerment is the need of the hour and teacher education should encourage the values of compassion, capacity to feel for others, to feel what it is like to grow under different-different circumstances; and to appreciate the human person, irrespective of sex, creed, colour or caste. It is then only that schools can create the conditions in which teachers as empowered actors can freely exercise their expert judgement, deal effectively with non-routine challenges, change school structure and in turn, depend on changed structures for self-advancement. However, the fulfilment of everything is possible only wher the teachers have awareness of values. Hence, if the teacher is full of 'sadguna', the future of the nation between a treasure of 'sadguna'. A teacher cultivates thousands of students by his or her 'Aacharana'. Hence, the professional ethics are only his or her power (samarthya) and because of these, he or she can gain self-respect, respect by other people (pupils, principals, parents and society) and same in the society. A teacher is, in fact, a kingpin in the implementation of any value-based education programme.

Concludingly, it may be said then that the teacher's empowerment needs to be completed on the basis of value-oriented programmes. They have to nurture and nurse the denominators of democracy, socialism and secularism. Useful training can only empower the teachers to function effectively and efficiently on desired level; and values enforce the teachers to choose their future dignity. Therefore, it is firmly staked here that value-based teacher-education programmes can only be able to empower the teachers. Being a source of emanating the paths of many progresses the teachers require be equipping and empowering with the value ingredients of teaching and learning, sacrifice, proficiency, accountability, responsibility, wisdom, vision and impartiality. Programmes developed on such values can surely empower the teachers; and a value-based teacher will deliver valuable outputs.

VALUE EDUCATION IN CONCLUSION

19

Prof. Kedar, Former Vice-Chancellor, Nagpur University, speaking at the Asian Educationalist's Conference on Human Rights and Education held at Brahma Kumari's Academy for a better world, warned that "There is no direct connection between values and technological progress. If there is, then, with the rise of technological and scientific knowledge, the values must also be at their peak. But it is not the situation today. Egotism, anger, violence, downfall of knowledge, wisdom, etc. are prevalent everywhere. Today's education simply increases the competitive spirit."

Value education, no doubt, is important; yet, it has become neglected subject area in today's classrooms and curriculum. However, value-education can be adequately addressed in both the classroom and college curriculum. A very convenient and successful way of communicating values to a person is through his or her education, whether in school, college or university level. Of course, learning is that process which continues right through a person's lifetime and values can be imbibed by a person through every experience and learning opportunity he or she gets. However, the ideal time to begin learning and imbibing values is right at the start of one's education, that may be in pre-school or in school. A good set of values will enable a person to raise his or her self-esteem, make others hold him or her in high respect and give him or her the confidence he or she requires to lead a life based on principles and self-confidence.

Most children start their education by attending a pre school institution, i.e., a play-school or a nursery. Children in such institutions, learn tolerance and cooperation. By mixing with children of their own age who might be from different strata of society, they learn how to be tolerant of one another, cooperate with one another and to be impartial in their dealings with one another.

Developing tolerance in a person from a young age will teach the person how to get along and live peacefully. In schools, the students can be taught discipline, punctuality, honesty, perseverance and patriotism. A student can the value and importance of discipline only when a certain code of conduct is enforced which a student has to adhere to.

Another effective way of communication (of values) in the classrooms is to correlate the content with other subjects, real-life experiences and past and present happenings. When the student relates his or her content with other subjects, it is easily retained. Also it is very easy and effective way of imbibing values in a student. Teacher must involve the students in discussions. This may not only create awareness among the students about our cultural and social values and traditions; but also creates tolerance and appreciation for our heritage. Also because the values are inculcated from childhood, they become a second nature as the child groups up.

In a simple way, it may be said that value education is education which teaches the following:

- How to live like well?
- How to find happiness?
- How to make others happy?
- How to manage all kinds of people and happiness well?
- How to grow and succeed in the right manner?

Historically, education, in countries all over the world has had two main goals — to help youngsters to master the skills of literacy and numeracy, i.e., academic education; and to help them build good character education, i.e., value education. Societies since the time of Plato have made character a deliberate aim of education. They understood that to create and maintain a civil society, there has to be education for character as well as intellect for democracy as well as literacy and for virtue as well as for skills and knowledge. Hence, fruitful education is the kind used for our welfare as well as that of others. This can only happen when one gets academic as well as value education.

Most effective way of communicating values is through narratives. Stories are interactive and therefore are very effective in communicating values.

- They teach by attraction rather than compulsion.
- They invite rather than impose.
- They capture the imagination and touch the heart.

These are, no doubt, the reasons why the world's greatest moral teachers have always used stories to teach eternal principles and truths. These are three ways in which stories can be used:

- Read and left without comment or discussion to do their own work.

- Read until a values issue is raised. At this point, the value issue is explored through discussion.
- Read through to the end and followed by a set of discussior questions.

Some examples where values touched the hearts of great people and turned them around can be taught in the discussions.

- Alfred Nobel: The scientist with a great deal of academic education, who invented explosives, was later on filled with remorse and guilt at his invention which could destroy hundreds of lives and level entire cities and cause pain and deformities even in future generations.
- Emperor Asoka was one of the greatest Indian rulers. But his early success was based on much violence. He reached the throne after killing nearly ninety kinsmen. One day, in the middle of the battle, he realised that there were no true victors in war because so many died on both sides. He became a follower of Buddha and changed his entire life. He served his people in wonderful ways. Even today, he is honoured and remembered.
- Adolf Hitler, the head of the German Empire, was at one time, the most powerful man on earth. He misused his powers to confiscate land and money that belonged to others and to torture and kill millions. He caused the Second World War. When defeat neared, he could face death bravely and committed suicide. His power deserted him when he needed it most because he had gained that power by throwing away all the good values from his life. His power was just an external show. It was not inner strength.

So far, whatever that has been discussed we do say and agree with the fact that education does help to impart values in education. Sometimes, we find that the values taught by parents have a negligible effect on children but if the same values are taught through education then the children readily accept the value and regard them as important. If we succeed in imparting these values to children, we can be sure that the Indians of the 21st century will be perfect citizens.

Thus, in order to create a better India, we should create citizens with moral values. Money once lost is not forever, but character once lost is lost forever. So we should all make efforts to preserve our character and this can be done only when we have the proper values. Values that are important for our moral and mental characteristics, that shape our character. The purpose of man is to live not only a life but a good life with moral values.

Family is probably the most powerful agent of value education in nearly all the societies. Certainly, it is the first and paramount influence on young children. It establishes role models, inculcates prejudices and offers a model of social hierarchy. School provides the most effective way for most modern societies to influence the attitude and belief of youth on a mass media. Within each country, specific institutions have special responsibility for providing value education. The degree of responsibility for value education by a particular institution will not be the same from one society to another and may change overtime within the same society. Each of these institutions gets affected; and one of the most important social institutions for value education is the school. Value education definitely gets greatly influenced by this social force! Value education is that process by which the school teaches the pupils the standards of correct behaviour.

In view of our glorious tradition of piety, tolerance, universal brotherhood with the present-day phenomenon of hypocracy, corruption, dishonestly and inhuman attitude, we are undoubtedly convinced that we are facing today the worst moral crisis. Mad race for higher standard of living had led to the worst degeneration in a value like honesty. Loyalty, courtsey and respect for elders, murders, dacoities, thefts and rapes have become common crime graph. And it may be firmly stated in this connection that there is serious defect in the school curriculum by showing the absence of provision for value education. It is hence the need of the day that our pupils must be taught both to understand and how to apply moral concepts and also to see the significance of behaving or not behaving in a consistent way that recognises the needs and interests of others. Hence, the need of the hour today is to organise the curriculum on value education in the interest of clarity and precision. Entire education must become a goal-directed activity. Accordingly, the broader objectives of the study may be stated as follows —

(i) To know the basis of value education such as philosophical, psychological, and sociological.

(ii) To trace the growth and development of value education in the international, national and state perspective.

(iii) To suggest measures for better utilisation of value education.

(iv) To clarify the meaning and concepts of value education.

(v) To evolve the evaluation criteria on value education.

(vi) To ascertain the extent of utilisation of value education in relation to plans, programmes and activities of value education.

(vii) To find out the interests of pupils in relation to different activities of value education.

The pattern of society that we find today is not conducive to freedom of thought. Today, we value reason and intellect, science and technology because they promise material affluence. We organise our social structure so that we can have bargaining power, not necessarily the power of the truth of the cause. In fact, everything is patterned with a view to further our material welfare. Under such a form of social order what we value most is not the individual in his or her fullness; but, the individual in relation to his or her material ease or hardship.

On the basis of the above said facts, value education must be such which will be able to develop the moral autonomy of the learner and also sensitivities of the value content of the school as well as classroom activities. The classroom activities should be free from attempt to indoctrinate the learner. For this, the pupils should be exposed to varieties of experiences and activities. This may include reading, listening, discussions, narration, direct presentation of ideas by the teacher and other strategies; and such strategies should be used with any of the following sources of value education.

— Biographies.

— Stories.

— Extracts from essays, articles, classics and newspapers.

— Parables, proverbs, quotations and poems.

— Value/moral dilemmas.

— Classroom incidents/anecdotes/conflicts.

Such sources can be used in many different ways to involve the pupils in thinking and reasoning about values.

The classroom teachers can themselves prepare action plans/lesson plans using these sources. Teaching is not a job; it is an attitude. Teacher is a source of information, a guide, a mentor, a surrogate parent, a motivator, all at the same time. Teaching is the only profession which always deals with the future. To be an ideal teacher, he or she has to be a role model. He or she should ask himself or herself —

Do I love my subject?

Do I love my profession?

Do I love my pupils as intensely as I love my own children?

Whatever that we have read so far, needless to say that a steep fall of values is witnessed during a century. Distortion of values is particularly due to imbalance between ancient values and explosion of knowledge in war field technology. Atomic weapons, bio-weapons, missiles, explosives, etc. are threatening the entire mankind. The developed countries possess all types of dreadful modern weapons and are trying to boss over developing and underdeveloped countries. Today, the entire mankind is living in the shade of fear. Man's very existence is at stake as he is indulging in wicked activities. Illegal marriages, prostitution, broken homes structure, divorce, etc. are also factors responsible for the decline of values. Lack of mutual concern between parents at home, dissatisfaction and lack of mutual concern between parents at home, lack of security in families are also the factors responsible for the erosion of values. It is very true that the living style of parents leave deep impressions on the minds of children.

At present, due to complexity of modern society there is no set of moral standards. Sense of responsibility and belongingness to a group has fully vanished. Mutual respect and consideration for others is disappearing. Social gatherings and group activities are organised without giving due weightage to values.

Values can be effectively included when they are a way of life of principal, teacher, and parents. Otherwise they remain theoretical. A value-based life transforms the individual into a person and a person into a human being.

On the basis of the above said facts, it may be said firmly that Value-Education, should constantly be taking place in the schools whether the teacher is conscious of it or not. Education is that process which brings about desirable changes of behaviour in the individual in his or her knowledge, skills, attitudes and values. The school seeks to achieve this through its curriculum that is nothing but the sum total of all its organisational activities.

Today's children are tomorrow's citizens. Children are the mirrors of innocence and reflect the values of our society. One should not forget the fact that:

"The child is the soul of the parents
The child is the ornament of home
The child is the glory of the garden
The child is the light of the family
The child is the smiling bud in our life."

Many a times, some such statement as follows, we do come across while going through the newspaper or newsletter – This reads as follows:

"In a span of three days, two school children and a college student ended their lives". Such occurrences, however seem to be inevitable, the way the high incidence of depression is afflicting today's young ones. The despondency created by examination stress, the failure to satisfy high parental expectations, the rising level of competition, the money crunch faced in trying to meet increasing peer demands, the increasing pressure on the time while attending various coaching classes and hobby classes even during vacations, are some of the factors which are causing a serious assault on the senses of our children. No wonder that some of them are led to feel that they have no alternative but to end their lives in order to escape the trauma. This situation which is worsening day by day, underlines the need to urgently have counselors in schools, who can retrieve our children from the start of despondency and give them courage and confidence to come our of the mental quagmire. The urgency to appoint counselors in schools in being emphasized by educationists from time to time, but governments have all along turned a deaf car to their plea. Hence, it is felt that the parents on their part should take the following steps:

(i) Allow the children to choose a career and study course, which is to their liking.

(ii) Try to remove the various fears that children may have nursed in their minds in their early childhood stage.

(iii) Avoid comparison with other children or their achievements.

(iv) Understand their mind by talking to them and making them speak out what they have in their minds.

The child do discuss the subject career choice with their peers but end up more confused and parents think that their children are not mature enough to take any major decision on their own. We must realize our students of Class X and XII are not sufficiently exposed to all practical realities of a career. They are captivated by the glamour. Hence, it is very essential that parents, teachers and education policy makers should come together to initiate an official decision to implement scientific planning of our children's careers.

Life is still going to be tougher in future. Hence, the best policy is to give full moral support to our children and boost their confidence in both themselves and the system in which they live.

The Secondary Education in India today is passing through the dive straits, it being treated like a forgotten middle. Emphasis is being given to Primary Education which gets major share of government funding which is fifty-two per cent whereas Secondary Education gets only 30% of this funding. This results in insufficient distribution of School infrastructure acute lack of trained teacher, inefficient teacher development, poor and dropping enrollment and inefficient overall funding for Schools. The scenario is really disturbing.

OUR TASK AHEAD: URGENCY AND PRIORITY

1. Introduction of human rights, peace, sustainable development and related subjects in School and College curriculum for the benefit of new generation.
2. Training of resource persons who can orient teachers and students.
3. Production of Instructional Materials and Teaching Aids in all regional languages to reach the millions in rural areas.
4. Celebration of Human Rights Day on Dec. 10 recognizing talented persons and for creating mass appeal.

People every where desire peace, progress, happiness, justice and security. To meet these desires, people look towards administrators, executives and managers as a ray of hope. An administrator has to be very sensitive to the expectations and appreciations of the public. The excellence in performance of an administrator is determined by the degree of satisfaction felt by the public.

It is irony that on one side we hope to make the world a better place to live in and on the other hand we indulge to corruption, vices, violence and other negative traits which lead to different crises, problems and challenges, under which the hope of happy world reduces to merely a day-dream. Consequently, tension and worries prevail all around.

We must realise and recognize that despite making all efforts to reap sweet results, we are declining day by day to deficiency in human values and virtues. They crying need of the time, therefore, is a renaissance of ethical, moral and spiritual values.

SETTING UP MANAGEMENT COURSES IN UNIVERSITY ADMINISTRATION: NEED OF THE TIME

Most universities in India are caught in an administrative mess. Some of them are sick needing urgent treatment. Some have become so unwieldy, they cannot manger their affairs with any semblance of efficiency. Some require bifurcation or even trifurcation. Until administrative charges are brought in, our universities may just continue rudderless with no one to show the right direction. What they need are managers to professionally govern them.

Vice-Chancellors are caught by group polities. They feel very lonely. The situation around them is frustrating. Naturally, they are obliged to lean on some group for moral and technical support. Morever, they do not feel free to take independent decisions lest they encroach upon someone's domain and fall from favour of politicians who pitch forked them to their coveted position.

The Registrars of universities whose status is equivalent to that of Professors generally do not have strong administrative background with the result that they tend to flounder and become slaves of the show-moving administrative system. No wonder, they become victims of vested interests and the inbuilt efficiency limitations.

The university's administrative staff is, with honorable exceptions, habituated in keeping matters pending for one reason or another. The various departments and sections dealing with matters like college affiliations, recognition of teachers and principals, college development council, university finance, registration of students for research degrees, statutory bodies like board of studies, academic council, senate, and most importantly the examination section, hardly work in proper coordination with each other.

The end result is: examinations are not held in time, the announcement of results get unduly delayed, leakage of question papers and malpractices in awarding marks become common occurrences, and convocations often get delayed disturbing the annual time table. Postponement of decision-making, often due to delay in processing, leads to various position in senate, academic council, management council, board of studies etc., remaining unfilled. Lack of advance planning aggravated by internal polities leaves many issues unsettled creating an atmosphere of seething discontent among students, teachers, parents and the public at large. The image of the university gets tarred irretrievably. It badly hurts the pride of the alumni who remember with nostalgia and gratitude the past glory of their alma mater.

The whole university administrative system presently appears to have deteriorated so much that mild palliatives will not work any more. A major reform by way redistribution of powers can alone rescue the system from the chronic malaise.

What the university administration needs is a Chief Executive Officer (CEO) with wide powers to implement the policy decisions of the Management Council backed by the order of the Vice-Chancellor and supported for implementation purposes by management degreeholders at the middle and lower levels of the administrative hierarchy.

It is time that academic bodies of the universities sit down to discuss the situation and evolve new courses, on the lines of hospital management courses, to train mangers for efficient functions of our universities. Serious urgent thinking following by action is the need of the time.

Really, it is time when all should realise the importance of love, peace and non-violence. The humanity is doomed without these value. Life is short and precious, and so it should be spent wisely, truthfully and happily.

A SELECT BIBLIOGRAPHY

1. Aggarwal J.C. : *Teacher and Education In a Developing Society,* Vikas House Pvt. Ltd., New Delhi, 1995.
2. Aggarwal J.C. : *Theory and Principles of Education,* Vikas House Pvt. Ltd., New Delhi, 1995.
3. Basantani K.T. : *Foundation Course On Social Awareness And Current Affairs,* Sheth Publishers.
4. Beck C, Mecoy N. and Bradley Commerson, J. : *Reflecting On Values,* O.I.S.E. Press, Toronto, 1980.
5. Beck C. : *Values and Living,* O.I.S.E. Press, Toroto, 1983.
6. Bengali M.D. : *Introduction to the World of Work,* Sheth Publishers, Bombay.
7. Bower W.C. : *The Curriculum of Religious Education,* Charles Seribner and Sons, New York, 1992.
8. Chitti Babu S.V. : Value-Orientation of Education University News, No. 18, Pp. 11-13, May 5, 1997.
9. Delors, Jacques (1996) : Learning the Treasures Within, UNESCO.
10. Dagar B.S. and Dhull Indira : A Case For Value-Oriented Education, University News, Vol. 35, No. 29, Pp. 10-11, July 21, 1997.
11. Gandhi K.L. : *Value-Education,* Gyan Publishing House, New Delhi, 1993.
12. Felix Coikara : Live Your Value-1990-Don Bosco Youth Animation Centre, Madras.
13. Ghosh A.K. : Moral Education, University News, Vol. 35, No. 44, Pp. 13-14, Nov. 3, 1997.
14. Government of India, Ministry of Education : Report of the Secondary Education Commission-1952-53, New Delhi by the Ministry, 1954.
15. Government of India, Ministry of Education : Report of the University Education Commission 1948-49, New Delhi by the Ministry, 1962.

16. Government of India, Ministry of Education : Report of the Committee on Religious and Moral Instruction (New Delhi by the Ministry), 1959.

17. Government of India, Ministry of India : Challenges of Education, A Policy Perspective, New Delhi, August 1986.

18. Government of India, Department of Education : National Policy on Education, 1986, Ministry of Human Resource Development, New Delhi, May 1986.

19. Goyal, B.R. : Documents on Social, Moral and Spiritual Values in Education, New Delhi, N.C.E.R.T., 1979.

20. Halstead: Mark and Taylor: Monica J. (2000) : "Learning and Teaching About Values. A Review of Recent Research" in Cambridge Journal of Education.

21. Inculcation of Ethical and Social Values in Teacher : Report of the working Group, N.C.E.R.T., 1982.

22. I.G.N.O.U., New Delhi : I.G.N.O.U. Teacher's Programme, University News, Pp. 17, May 27, 1991.

23. Krishnamurti J. : 1956 Educational Significance of Life- London, Victor-Gollanez.

24. Mascarenhas M. and Justa H.R. : Value-Education in School and Other Essays, Konark Publications Ltd.

25. Mc Millan : Moral Science Series, Macmillan and Co. Ltd., Bombay, 1961.

26. National Commission for Value Education : University News: XXX No. 30, 1992.

27. National Policy on Education : 1986 — MHRD

28. National Council of Education Research and Training : Education Commission (1965-66).

29. Passi B.K. and Singh Prabhakar : Value Education, National Psychological Corporation, Agra, 1961.

30. Rama Rao K. : Moral Education — A Practical Approach, Ramkrishna Institute of Moral Education, Yadavgiri, Mysore — 1956.

31. Report of the Core Group on Value Orientation of Education Planning Commission : Government of India, New Delhi, 1992.

32. Report of the Working Group to Review Teachers Training Programme : (In the light of the need for value-orientaion), Ministry of Education and Culture, Government of India, New Delhi, 1983.

33. Ruhela S.P. : Value-Orientation of Teacher Education Curriculum In Indian Human Values and Education, New Delhi, Sterling Publishers Pvt. Ltd., 1986

34. Ruhela Satya Pal : Human Values and Education, Sterling Publishers Pvt. Ltd., 1986.

35. Sarangi Radhashyam : Moral Education in Schools, Deep and Deep Publishers, New Delhi.

36. Saraswati S. : A New National Policy for Youth, The HINDU, 19th Nov., 1996.

37. Shetty Anita, Khirwadkar Anjali, Tomar Archana : Value Education — Need of the Present Generation, University News, Vol. 35, No. 41, Pp. 12-4, Oct., 13, 1997.

38. Sr. M. Linus A.C. : Edited, St. Anne's College of Education, Mangalore, 1994.

39. Shetty Anita and Pushpanadham K. : Valuing Values, University News, Vol. 35, No. 52, Pp. 7-9, December 29, 1997.

40. Singh R.P. : Teacher Education in India, An Appraisal, Progressive Education Herald, Vol. 6, No. 1, 1991.

41. Sidney Simon, Lenald House, Howard Krischenlaum : Value Clarification, Hard Publication Co., New York, 1972.

42. Techniques of Teaching Values : University News, Vol. XXVI, No. 33, 1988.

43. Tomilnson P. and Quniton M. : Value Across the Curriculum, The Falmer Press, London.

44. Traclks for Living : Value Education,. National Workshop, 1979, Super Publishers, IV/85, Chandni Chowk, New Delhi 110 016.

45. Value-Orientation to Education : Report of the Conference of Deans of Education, NCERT, 1986.

46. Varma S.K. : Value in Education or Education for Values, University News, July, 1991, New Delhi.

47. Yogendra Singh : Modernisation of Indian Tradition: Thompson Press, 1974, New Delhi.

48. Yahn, Huby, Peterson, Patricia and Thomas Murrad (1998) : Teachers' views an Moral Education In Taiwan and the U.S.A. in International Review of Education.